Library Training for Staff and Customers

Library Training for Staff and Customers has been co-published simultaneously as *Journal of Library Administration,* Volume 29, Number 1 1999.

The *Journal of Library Administration* Monographic "Separates"

Below is a list of "separates," which in serials librarianship means a special issue simultaneously published as a special journal issue or double-issue *and* as a "separate" hardbound monograph. (This is a format which we also call a "DocuSerial.")

"Separates" are published because specialized libraries or professionals may wish to purchase a specific thematic issue by itself in a format which can be separately cataloged and shelved, as opposed to purchasing the journal on an on-going basis. Faculty members may also more easily consider a "separate" for classroom adoption.

"Separates" are carefully classified separately with the major book jobbers so that the journal tie-in can be noted on new book order slips to avoid duplicate purchasing.

You may wish to visit Haworth's website at . . .

http://www.haworthpressinc.com

. . . to search our online catalog for complete tables of contents of these separates and related publications.

You may also call 1-800-HAWORTH (outside US/Canada: 607-722-5857), or Fax 1-800-895-0582 (outside US/Canada: 607-771-0012), or e-mail at:

getinfo@haworthpressinc.com

Library Training for Staff and Customers, edited by Sara Ramser Beck, BA, MLS, MBA (Vol. 29, No. 1, 1999). *This comprehensive book is designed to assist library professionals involved in presenting or planning training for library staff members and customers. You will explore ideas for effective general reference training, training on automated systems, training in specialized subjects such as African American history and biography, and training for areas such as patents and trademarks, and business subjects.* Library Training for Staff and Customers *answers numerous training questions and is an excellent guide for planning staff development.*

Collection Development in the Electronic Environment, edited by Sul H. Lee (Vol. 28, No. 4, 1999). *Through case studies and firsthand experiences, this volume discusses meeting the needs of scholars at universities, budgeting issues, user education, staffing in the electronic age, collaborating libraries and resources, and how vendors meet the needs of different customers.*

The Age Demographics of Academic Librarians: A Professor Apart, edited by Stanley J. Wilder (Vol. 28, No. 3, 1999). *The average age of librarians has been increasing dramatically since 1990. This unique book will provide insights on how this demographic issue can impact a library and what can be done to make the effects positive.*

Collection Development in a Digital Environment, edited by Sul H. Lee (Vol. 28, No. 1, 1999). *Explores ethical and technological dilemmas of collection development and gives several suggestions on how a library can successfully deal with these challenges and provide patrons with the information they need.*

Scholarship, Research Libraries, and Global Publishing, by Jutta Reed-Scott (Vol. 27, No. 3/4, 1999). *This book documents a research project in conjunction with the Association of Research Libraries (ARL) that explores the issue of foreign acquisition and how it affects collection in international studies, area studies, collection development, and practices of international research libraries.*

Managing Multiculturalism and Diversity in the Library: Principles and Issues for Administrators, edited by Mark Winston (Vol. 27, No. 1/2, 1999). *Defines diversity, clarifies why it is important to address issues of diversity; and identifies goals related to diversity and how to go about achieving those goals.*

Information Technology Planning, edited by Lori A. Goetsch (Vol. 26, No. 3/4, 1999). *Offers innovative approaches and strategies useful in your library and provides some food for thought about information technology as we approach the millennium.*

The Economics of Information in the Networked Environment, edited by Meredith A. Butler, MLS, and Bruce R. Kingma, PhD (Vol. 26, No. 1/2, 1998). *"A book that should be read both by information professionals and by administrators, faculty and others who share a collective concern to provide the most information to the greatest number at the lowest cost in the networked environment." (Thomas J. Galvin, PhD, Professor of Information Science and Policy, University at Albany, State University of New York)*

OCLC 1967-1997: Thirty Years of Furthering Access to the World's Information, edited by K. Wayne Smith (Vol. 25, No. 2/3/4, 1998). *"A rich–and poignantly personal, at times–historical account of what is surely one of this century's most important developments in librarianship." (Deanna B. Marcum, PhD, President, Council on Library and Information Resources, Washington, DC)*

Management of Library and Archival Security: From the Outside Looking In, edited by Robert K. O'Neill, PhD (Vol. 25, No. 1, 1998). *"Provides useful advice and on-target insights for professionals caring for valuable documents and artifacts." (Menzi L Behrnd-Klodt, JD, Attorney/Archivist, Klodt and Associates, Madison, WI)*

Economics of Digital Information: Collection, Storage, and Delivery, edited by Sul H. Lee (Vol. 24, No. 4, 1997). *Highlights key concepts and issues vital to a library's successful venture into the digital environment and helps you understand why the transition from the printed page to the digital packet has been problematic for both creators of proprietary materials and users of those materials.*

The Academic Library Director: Reflections on a Position in Transition, edited by Frank D'Andraia, MLS (Vol. 24, No. 3, 1997). *"A useful collection to have whether you are seeking a position as director or conducting a search for one." (College & Research Libraries News)*

Emerging Patterns of Collection Development in Expanding Resource Sharing, Electronic Information, and Network Environment, edited by Sul H. Lee (Vol. 24, No. 1/2, 1997). *"The issues it deals with are common to us all. We all need to make our finds go further and our resources work harder, and there are ideas here which we can all develop." (The Library Association Record)*

Interlibrary Loan/Document Delivery and Customer Satisfaction: Strategies for Redesigning Services, edited by Pat L. Weaver-Meyers, Wilbur A. Stolt, Yem S. Fong (Vol. 23, No. 1/2, 1997). *"No interlibrary loan department supervisor at any mid-sized to large college or university library can afford not to read this book." (Gregg Sapp, MLS, MEd, Head of Access Services, University of Miami, Richter Library, Coral Gables, Florida)*

Access, Resource Sharing and Collection Development, edited by Sul H. Lee (Vol. 22, No. 4, 1996). *Features continuing investigation and discussion of important library issues, specifically the role of libraries in acquiring, storing, and disseminating information in different formats.*

Managing Change in Academic Libraries, edited by Joseph J. Branin (Vol. 22, No. 2/3, 1996). *"Touches on several aspects of academic library management, emphasizing the changes that are occurring at the present time. . . . Recommended this title for individuals or libraries interested in management aspects of academic libraries." (RQ American Library Association)*

Libraries and Student Assistants: Critical Links, edited by William K. Black, MLS (Vol. 21, No. 3/4, 1995). *"A handy reference work on many important aspects of managing student assistants. . . . Solid, useful information on basic management issues in this work and several chapters are useful for experienced managers." (The Journal of Academic Librarianship)*

The Future of Resource Sharing, edited by Shirley K. Baker and Mary E. Jackson, MLS (Vol. 21, No. 1/2, 1995). *"Recommended for library and information science schools because of its balanced presentation of the ILL/document delivery issues." (Library Acquisitions: Practice and Theory)*

The Future of Information Services, edited by Virginia Steel, MA, and C. Brigid Welch, MLS (Vol. 20, No. 3/4, 1995). *"The leadership discussions will be useful for library managers as will the discussions of how library structures and services might work in the next century." (Australian Special Libraries)*

The Dynamic Library Organizations in a Changing Environment, edited by Joan Giesecke, MLS, DPA (Vol. 20, No. 2, 1995). *"Provides a significant look at potential changes in the library world and presents its readers with possible ways to address the negative results of such changes.... Covers the key issues facing today's libraries... Two thumbs up!" (Marketing Library Resources)*

Access, Ownership, and Resource Sharing, edited by Sul H. Lee, PhD (Vol. 20, No. 1, 1995). *The contributing authors present a useful and informative look at the current status of information provision and some of the challenges the subject presents.*

Planning for Library Services: A Guide to Utilizing Planning Methods for Library Management, edited by Charles R. McClure, PhD (Vol. 2, No. 3/4, 1982). *"Should be read by anyone who is involved in planning processes of libraries–certainly by every administrator of a library or system." (American Reference Books Annual)*

Libraries as User-Centered Organizations: Imperatives for Organizational Change, edited by Meredith A. Butler (Vol. 19, No. 3/4, 1994). *"Presents a very timely and well-organized discussion of major trends and influences causing organizational changes." (Science Books & Films)*

Declining Acquisitions Budgets: Allocation, Collection Development and Impact Communication, edited by Sul H. Lee (Vol. 19, No. 2, 1994). *"Expert and provocative.... Presents many ways of looking at library budget deterioration and responses to it... There is much food for thought here. "(Library Resources & Technical Services)*

The Role and Future of Special Collections in Research Libraries: British and American Perspectives, edited by Sul H. Lee (Vol. 19, No. 1, 1993). *"A provocative but informative read for library users, academic administrators, and private sponsors." (International Journal of Information and Library Research)*

Catalysts for Change: Managing Libraries in the 1990s, edited by Gisela M. von Dran, DPA, MLS, and Jennifer Cargill, MSLS, MSed (Vol. 18, No. 3/4, 1994). *"A useful collection of articles which focuses on the need for librarians to employ enlightened management practices in order to adapt to, and thrive, in the rapidly changing information environment." (Australian Library Review)*

Integrating Total Quality Management in a Library Setting, edited by Susan Jurow, MLS, and Susan B. Barnard, MLS (Vol. 18, No. 1/2, 1993). *"Especially valuable are the librarian experiences that directly relate to real concerns about TQM. Recommended for all professional reading collections." (Library Journal)*

Leadership in Academic Libraries: Proceedings of the W. Porter Kellam Conference, The University of Georgia, May 7, 1991, edited by William Gray Potter (Vol. 17, No. 4, 1993). *"Will be of interest to those concerned with the history of American academic libraries." (Australian Library Review)*

Collection Assessment and Acquisitions Budgets, edited by Sul H. Lee (Vol. 17, No. 2, 1993). *Contains timely information about the assessment of academic library collections and the relationship of collection assessment to acquisition budgets.*

Developing Library Staff for the 21st Century, edited by Maureen Sullivan (Vol. 17, No. 1, 1992). *"I found myself enthralled with this highly readable publication. It is one of those rare compilations that manages to successfully integrate current general management operational thinking in the context of academic library management." (Bimonthly Review of Law Books)*

Vendor Evaluation and Acquisition Budgets, edited by Sul H. Lee (Vol. 16, No. 3, 1992). *"The title doesn't do justice to the true scope of this excellent collection of papers delivered at the sixth annual conference on library acquisitions sponsored by the University of Oklahoma Libraries." (Kent K. Hendrickson, BS, MALS, Dean of Libraries, University of Nebraska-Lincoln) Find insight discussions on the impact of rising costs on library budgets and management in this groundbreaking book.*

The Management of Library and Information Studies Education, edited by Herman L. Totten, PhD, MLS (Vol. 16 No. 1/2, 1992). *"Offers something of interest to everyone connected with LIS education–the undergraduate contemplating a master's degree, the doctoral student struggling with courses and career choices, the new faculty member aghast at conflicting responsibilities, the experienced but stressed LIS professor, and directors of LIS Schools."* *(Education Libraries)*

Library Management in the Information Technology Environment: Issues, Policies, and Practice for Administrators, edited by Brice G. Hobrock, PhD, MLS (Vol. 15, No. 3/4, 1992). *"A road map to identify some of the alternative routes to the electronic library."* *(Stephen Rollins, Associate Dean for Library Services, General library, University of New Mexico)*

Managing Technical Services in the 90's, edited by Drew Racine (Vol. 15, No. 1/2, 1991). *"Presents an eclectic overview of the challenges currently facing all library technical services efforts. . . . Recommended to library administrators and interested practitioners."* *(Library Journal)*

Budgets for Acquisitions: Strategies for Serials, Monographs, and Electronic Formats, edited by Sul Lee (Vol. 14, No. 3, 1991). *"Much more than a series of handy tips for the careful shopper. This [book] is a most useful one–well-informed, thought-provoking, and authoritative."* *(Australian Library Review)*

Creative Planning for Library Administration: Leadership for the Future, edited by Kent Hendrickson, MALS (Vol. 14, No. 2, 1991). *"Provides some essential information on the planning process, and the mix of opinions and methodologies, as well as examples relevant to every library manager, resulting in a very readable foray into a topic too long avoided by many of us."* *(Canadian Library Journal)*

Strategic Planning in Higher Education: Implementing New Roles for the Academic Library, edited by James F. Williams, II, MLS (Vol. 13, No. 3/4, 1991). *"A welcome addition to the sparse literature on strategic planning in university libraries. Academic librarians considering strategic planning for their libraries will learn a great deal from this work."* *(Canadian Library Journal)*

Personnel Administration in an Automated Environment, edited by Philip E. Leinbach, MLS (Vol. 13 No. 1/2, 1990). *"An interesting and worthwhile volume, recommended to university library administrators and to others interested in thought-provoking discussion of the personnel implications of automation."* *(Canadian Library Journal)*

Library Development: A Future Imperative, edited by Dwight F. Burlingame, PhD (Vol. 12, No. 4, 1990). *"This volume provides an excellent overview of fundraising with special application to libraries. . . . A useful book that is highly recommended for all libraries."* *(Library Journal)*

Library Material Costs and Access to Information, edited by Sul Lee (Vol. 12, No. 3, 1991). *"A cohesive treatment of the issue. Although the book's contributors possess a research library perspective, the data and the ideas presented are of interest and benefit to the entire profession, especially academic librarians."* *(Library Resources and Technical Services)*

Training Issues and Strategies in Libraries, edited by Paul M. Gherman, MALS, and Frances O. Painter, MLS, MBA (Vol. 12, No. 2, 1990). *"There are . . . useful chapters, all by different authors, each with a preliminary summary of the content–a device that saves much time in deciding whether to read the whole chapter or merely skim through it. Many of the chapters are essentially practical without too much emphasis on theory. This book is a good investment."* *(Library Association Record)*

Library Education and Employer Expectations, edited by E. Dale Cluff, PhD, MLS (Vol. 11, No. 3/4, 1990). *"Useful to library school students and faculty interested in employment problems and employer perspectives. Librarians concerned with recruitment practices will also be interested."* *(Information Technology and Libraries)*

Managing Public Libraries in the 21st Century, edited by Pat Woodrum, MLS (Vol. 11, No. 1/2, 1989). *"A broad-based collection of topics that explores the management problems and possibilities public libraries will be facing in the 21st century. "(Robert Swisher, PhD, Director, School of Library and Information Studies, The University of Oklahoma)*

Human Resources Management in Libraries, edited by Gisela M. Webb, MLS, MPA (Vol. 10, No. 4, 1989). *"Thought provoking and enjoyable reading. . . . Provides valuable insights for the effective information manager." (Special Libraries)*

Creativity, Innovation, and Entrepreneurship in Libraries, edited by Donald E. Riggs, EdD, MLS (Vol. 10, No. 2/3, 1989). *"The volume is well worth reading as a whole. . . . There is very little repetition, and it should stimulate thought." (Australian Library Review)*

The Impact of Rising Costs of Serials and Monographs on Library Services and Programs, edited by Sul H. Lee (Vol. 10, No. 1, 1989). *". . . Sul Lee hit a winner here." (Serials Review)*

Computing, Electronic Publishing, and Information Technology: Their Impact on Academic Libraries, edited by Robin N. Downes (Vol. 9, No. 4, 1989). *"For a relatively short and easily digestible discussion of these issues this book can be recommended, not only to those in academic libraries, but also to those in similar types of library or information unit, and to academics and educators in the field." (Journal of Documentation)*

Library Management and Technical Services: The Changing Role of Technical Services in Library Organizations, edited by Jennifer Cargill, MSLS, MSed (Vol. 9, No. 1, 1988). *"As a practical and instructive guide to issues such as automation, personnel matters, education, management techniques and liaison with other services, senior library managers with a sincere interest in evaluating the role of their technical services should find this a timely publication." (Library Association Record)*

Management Issues in the Networking Environment, edited by Edward R. Johnson, PhD (Vol. 8, No. 3/4, 1989). *"Particularly useful for librarians/information specialists contemplating establishing a local network." (Australian Library Review)*

Acquisitions, Budgets, and Material Costs: Issues and Approaches, edited by Sul H. Lee (Supp. #2, 1988). *"The advice of these library practitioners is sensible and their insights illuminating for librarians in academic libraries." (American Reference Books Annual)*

Pricing and Costs of Monographs and Serials: National and International Issues, edited by Sul H. Lee (Supp. #1, 1987). *"Eminently readable. There is a good balance of chapters on serials and monographs and the perspective of suppliers, publishers, and library practitioners are presented. A book well worth reading." (Australasian College Libraries)*

Legal Issues for Library and Information Managers, edited by William Z. Nasri, JD, PhD (Vol. 7, No. 4, 1987). *"Useful to any librarian looking for protection or wondering where responsibilities end and liabilities begin. Recommended." (Academic Library Book Review)*

Archives and Library Administration: Divergent Traditions and Common Concerns, edited by Lawrence J. McCrank, PhD, MLS (Vol. 7, No. 2/3, 1986). *"A forward-looking view of archives and libraries. . . . Recommend[ed] to students, teachers, and practitioners alike of archival and library science. It is readable, thought-provoking, and provides a summary of the major areas of divergence and convergence." (Association of Canadian Map Libraries and Archives)*

Excellence in Library Management, edited by Charlotte Georgi, MLS, and Robert Bellanti, MLS, MBA (Vol. 6, No. 3, 1985). *"Most beneficial for library administrators . . . for anyone interested in either library/information science or management." (Special Libraries)*

Marketing and the Library, edited by Gary T. Ford (Vol. 4, No. 4, 1984). *Discover the latest methods for more effective information dissemination and learn to develop successful programs for specific target areas.*

Finance Planning for Libraries, edited by Murray S. Martin (Vol. 3, No. 3/4, 1983). *Stresses the need for libraries to weed out expenditures which do not contribute to their basic role–the collection and organization of information–when planning where and when to spend money.*

Library Training for Staff and Customers

Sara Ramser Beck
Editor

Library Training for Staff and Customers has been co-published simultaneously as *Journal of Library Administration,* Volume 29, Number 1 1999.

The Haworth Information Press
An Imprint of
The Haworth Press, Inc.
New York • London • Oxford

Published by

The Haworth Information Press, 10 Alice Street, Binghamton, NY 13904-1580 USA

The Haworth Information Press is an imprint of The Haworth Press, Inc., 10 Alice Street, Binghamton, NY 13904-1580 USA.

Library Training for Staff and Customers has been co-published simultaneously as *Journal of Library Administration,* Volume 29, Number 1 1999.

Cover design by Thomas J. Mayshock Jr.

Library of Congress Cataloging-in-Publication Data

Library training for staff and customers / Sara Ramser Beck, editor.
        p. cm.
        Co-published simultaneously as Journal of Library Administration, volume 29, no. 1, 1999.
        Includes bibliographical references and index.
        ISBN 0-7890-0965-X (alk. paper)–ISBN 0-7890-0983-8 (pbk : alk. paper)
        1. Reference services (Libraries)–Study and teaching–United States. I. Beck, Sara Ramser.
Z711.2 .L7337 2000
025.5′2′–071073–dc21   00-023133

INDEXING & ABSTRACTING

Contributions to this publication are selectively indexed or abstracted in print, electronic, online, or CD-ROM version(s) of the reference tools and information services listed below. This list is current as of the copyright date of this publication. See the end of this section for additional notes.

- *Academic Abstracts/CD-ROM*
- *Academic Search: data base of 2,000 selected academic serials, updated monthly*
- *AGRICOLA Database*
- *BUBL Information Service, an Internet-based Information Service for the UK higher education community <URL: http://bubl.ac.uk/>*
- *Cambridge Scientific Abstracts*
- *CNPIEC Reference Guide: Chinese National Directory of Foreign Periodicals*
- *Current Articles on Library Literature and Services (CALLS)*
- *Current Awareness Abstracts of Library & Information Management Literature, ASLIB (UK)*
- *Current Index to Journals in Education*
- *Educational Administration Abstracts (EAA)*
- *FINDEX, free Internet Directory of over 150,000 publications from around the world (www.publist.com)*
- *Higher Education Abstracts*
- *IBZ International Bibliography of Periodical Literature*
- *Index to Periodical Articles Related to Law*
- *Information Reports & Bibliographies*
- *Information Science Abstracts*
- *Informed Librarian, The*
- *INSPEC*
- *Journal of Academic Librarianship: Guide to Professional Literature, The*

(continued)

- *Konyvtari Figyelo-Library Review*
- *Library & Information Science Abstracts (LISA)*
- *Library and Information Science Annual (LISCA)*
- *Library Literature*
- *MasterFILE: updated database from EBSCO Publishing*
- *Newsletter of Library and Information Services*
- *OT BibSys*
- *PAIS (Public Affairs Information Service) NYC (www.pais.org)*
- *PASCAL, c/o Institute de L'Information Scientifique et Technique*
- *Referativnyi Zhurnal (Abstracts Journal of the All-Russian Institute of Scientific and Technical Information)*
- *Trade & Industry Index*

Special Bibliographic Notes related to special journal issues (separates) and indexing/abstracting:

- indexing/abstracting services in this list will also cover material in any "separate" that is co-published simultaneously with Haworth's special thematic journal issue or DocuSerial. Indexing/abstracting usually covers material at the article/chapter level.
- monographic co-editions are intended for either non-subscribers or libraries which intend to purchase a second copy for their circulating collections.
- monographic co-editions are reported to all jobbers/wholesalers/approval plans. The source journal is listed as the "series" to assist the prevention of duplicate purchasing in the same manner utilized for books-in-series.
- to facilitate user/access services all indexing/abstracting services are encouraged to utilize the co-indexing entry note indicated at the bottom of the first page of each article/chapter/contribution.
- this is intended to assist a library user of any reference tool (whether print, electronic, online, or CD-ROM) to locate the monographic version if the library has purchased this version but not a subscription to the source journal.
- individual articles/chapters in any Haworth publication are also available through the Haworth Document Delivery Service (HDDS).

Library Training
for Staff and Customers

CONTENTS

ABOUT THE EDITOR

Sara Ramser Beck, BA, MLS, MBA, is Manager of the Business, Science, and Technology Department at the St. Louis Public Library in Missouri. Ms. Beck has also worked in public service positions at Washington University, the University of Missouri, St. Louis, and in the Acquisitions Department at St. Louis University and Kent State University. She is an active member of the American Library Association and has served on the Business Reference in Public Libraries and Copyright committees. Ms. Beck is an active member of the Special Libraries Association, where she has held many offices, including President in the St. Louis Metropolitan Area Chapter. A prolific writer, Ms. Beck has written articles for a variety of publications, including a monthly newspaper column on library resources for the *Canton Repository.*

More Than Meets the Eye:
Management Support for Reference Service and Training

Ralph Gers
Nancy Bolin

SUMMARY. Reference service delivery requires informed managerial involvement. This article offers a rationale for public libraries' being in the information service business, discusses reference service performance, and addresses behavior-specific training. The most effective models of training and transfer of training are presented. Information on the "Effective Reference Performance" workshop for reference interview skills is offered as an example incorporating these models. The role of the manager/administrator, before, during and after the training, directly affects skills maintenance and effective reference performance over time. *[Article copies available for a fee from The Haworth Document Delivery Service: 1-800-342-9678. E-mail address: getinfo@haworthpressinc.com <Website: http://www.haworthpressinc.com>]*

KEYWORDS. Reference, management, training, surveys, information services, skills training, transfer of training, model reference behaviors, effective reference performance

---

Ralph Gers and Nancy Bolin are principals of Transform, Inc., Columbia, Maryland, a training, surveying, and consulting firm. Previously, both worked at the Division of Library Development and Services, Maryland State Department of Education, Baltimore, Maryland. Ralph Gers holds an MLS degree from Rutgers University, and Nancy Bolin holds an MALS degree from the University of Michigan-Ann Arbor and a Specialist's degree in Gerontology and Library Science from the University of Wisconsin-Madison.

[Haworth co-indexing entry note]: "More Than Meets the Eye: Management Support for Reference Service and Training." Gers, Ralph, and Nancy Bolin. Co-published simultaneously in *Journal of Library Administration* (The Haworth Information Press, an imprint of The Haworth Press, Inc.) Vol. 29, No. 1, 1999, pp. 1-15; and: *Library Training for Staff and Customers* (ed: Sara Ramser Beck) The Haworth Information Press, an imprint of The Haworth Press, Inc., 2000, pp. 1-15. Single or multiple copies of this article are available for a fee from The Haworth Document Delivery Service [1-800-342-9678, 9:00 a.m. - 5:00 p.m. (EST). E-mail address: getinfo@haworthpressinc.com].

1

The delivery of information services–spanning an almost limitless variety of subjects–is a unique service offered by most public libraries. Managing the delivery of this service is one of the most important jobs a manager undertakes. Competent reference service goes beyond providing staff, materials, and a place for the delivery of the service.

INFORMATION SERVICES AS A PUBLIC LIBRARY FUNCTION

In the mid-1970s, the Division of Library Development (DLDS) of the Maryland State Department of Education managed two major surveys of people's information needs conducted in eight counties on the Eastern Shore by Annapolis Research, Inc.,[1] and in the three counties of Southern Maryland by Westat, Inc.[2] These surveys investigated information needed to help solve problems, to become informed about general subjects, to pursue entertainment activities, to assist in formal education, and to assist in self education. When asked to place these needs in priority order, the respondents ranked information needed to help solve problems highest.

In the 1980s a series of surveys was conducted in seventeen counties throughout the state of Maryland by the Survey Research Center of the University of Maryland, regarding people's problem-related information needs. Based on 6,828 respondents, the data showed that, for all problems across all sources of information used (except the public library) people received a complete answer to their question/problem only thirty-nine percent of the time. When people used the public library as a source of information, they received a complete answer forty-three percent of the time. Thus, the public library provides complete answers to questions/problems that people have more often than all other sources combined. Granted, providing complete answers to people's problem-related questions forty-three percent of the time is not as high a level of performance as one might like to see; however, the data clearly showed that public libraries are the best source of information available!

These data provide a rationale for public libraries' being in the information business. They perform better than all other sources of information available. Indeed, the survey data showed that they even perform slightly better than health professionals dealing with health-related questions!

In 1981, DLDS managed a massive study[3] of materials availability and user satisfaction. Surveying sixty public library outlets during sample days in October, 1981, a data base of 25,000 respondents was gathered, using trained interviewers. Of the people who were looking for information on a subject, only forty-five percent of them received complete answers to their questions. These questions were much broader than the problem-related questions addressed in the other studies mentioned above. However, it is interesting to note that the "success rates" were very similar.

REFERENCE SERVICE PERFORMANCE

In 1983, the DLDS conducted its first state-wide unobtrusive reference survey in which forty questions (twenty walk-in and twenty phone-in) were presented at sixty public library outlets (a stratified random sample of Maryland's 156 outlets at that time). These questions were only "moderately difficult." Only fifty-five percent of these were answered completely and correctly. The results were reported in *Library Journal* in 1985.[4]

In a fall, 1983 article in *RQ*,[5] Terence Crowley summarized the results of several unobtrusive reference surveys conducted by various researchers throughout the United States and concluded that public libraries are providing only half-right reference.

In 1986, an article in *Library Journal*[6] by Peter Hernon and Charles McClure goes so far as to state, "[Rules can be] proposed that reference staff in academic and public libraries, regardless of department, correctly answer approximately fifty-five percent of the factual and bibliographic questions they receive." Transform, Inc. conducts unobtrusive reference surveys for clients, and based upon surveys as recent as 1997, it would appear that, for libraries whose staff have not been trained in the Model Reference Behaviors, half-right reference is still the norm.

Over the years, since these results have appeared, there appears to have been only limited concern among library administrators in the United States about the problem of providing incomplete and/or incorrect information to library customers.

Why hasn't there been more of a concern? As part of Transform, Inc.'s reference training workshops, administrators and reference managers are asked how well they think their reference staff are doing and most reply that they are providing complete and correct answers–eighty percent or ninety percent of the time. When unobtrusive surveys have been conducted in these managers' libraries, the data revealed that their libraries were providing only half-right reference or worse (and the data reflect questions to which it would be considered easy to find the answers).

For example, Table 1 lists the eleven hardest questions in the 1983 survey. The fourth column lists the questions by whether they were direct or escalator questions. The term "escalator" was coined by Thomas Childers.[7] A direct question is a question that is asked directly, e.g., #6 was a direct, walk-in question. The surrogate interviewer walked into the library, to the reference desk, and asked directly, "Can you tell me who referred to second marriages as the victory of hope over experience?" An escalator question is a question that is first presented as a broad question; then, if the librarian probes, the surrogate interviewer escalates to the more specific level; then if the librarian probes further, the interviewer escalates to the most specific level for which an answer is sought. For example, #40 was an escalator walk-in question. The interviewer asked, "Do you have any books on dogs?" If the librarian probed, perhaps by asking, "What kind of information on dogs are you looking for?" the interviewer would respond, "I'm interested in breeds of dogs." If the librarian probed further, perhaps by asking, "Could you be more specific?" the interviewer would respond, "I want to know if the West Highland Terrier is a breed of dog registered with the American Kennel Club."

In 1983, before librarians in Maryland were trained in the Model Reference Behaviors, only 18.3% of the sixty libraries provided a complete and correct answer to question #40, "Can you tell me if the West Highland Terrier is a breed of dog registered with the AKC?" This is not a hard question. The data in the table reveal that escalator questions are the most difficult questions to answer, primarily because most librarians do not use open probes to discover the customer's specific question. The best searching skills are of little value if the librarian does not discover the customer's specific question for which an answer is sought.

This is important because perhaps fifty percent of questions asked in public libraries are broadly phrased when first presented. Indeed, in a 1996 pilot study by Transform, Inc., of reference service to children in Maryland public libraries, fully sixty-seven percent of children's initial questions were broadly phrased when first presented to the librarians. The results were reported[8] at the American Library Association Annual Conference in San Francisco in 1997. In investigating how well reference staff do in answering reference questions, the data suggest that at least fifty percent of the questions posed should be escalator questions. In the 1986 and 1990 state-wide surveys in Maryland, eight out of eleven hardest questions to answer also were escalator questions. In the 1994 survey, seven of the eleven hardest questions were escalator questions.

In their 1986 article[9] Hernon and McClure state, "For approximately twenty years now, the library community has been aware of the fifty-five percent accuracy rate, yet few tangible ongoing strategies have been developed to address this finding." In Crowley's article,[10] he asks, "What changes in library training, policy, and practice can help us improve public service?"

THE EMPIRICAL BASE OF TRAINING
IN THE MODEL REFERENCE BEHAVIORS

In the 1983 state-wide study, in addition to measuring whether librarians provided complete and correct answers to questions posed to them, the survey also measured what behaviors reference staff used. Analysis of the data showed that of the more than thirty behaviors measured, about twenty of them were positively correlated with the provision of complete and correct answers. These behaviors were named the Model Reference Behaviors.

In 1984 and 1985, seventeen library outlets were trained by staff at DLDS in the application of these behaviors, with each participant going through three full days of training and receiving many opportunities to practice using the skills. Most of the participants engaged in peer coaching after the training to help transfer the behaviors to the job. The results were reported[11] at the Public Library Association National Conference in St. Louis in early 1986.

In 1986, DLDS conducted another state-wide reference survey, in the same libraries as in the 1983 study, using comparable questions. This time, they had a pre-test, post-test experimental design, with a treatment group and a comparison group. The trained librarians performed much, much better than untrained librarians. Analysis of the variables showed that difference in performance was due to the training. The results were reported[12] at the Public Library Association National Conference in Pittsburgh in 1988.

In 1990, DLDS hired Transform, Inc. to conduct another state-wide survey. This time eighty-seven library outlets participated, yielding a data base of 3,480 questions. In addition to investigating reference performance and the use of the Model Reference Behaviors (MRB's), Transform also was charged with investigating the impact of training, peer coaching, and support activities.

Looking at all the strategies used to support the continued use of the MRB's, the results showed:

- Most important was that at least three days of training be provided, with sufficient time for participants to learn and practice the behaviors. The major element of the training was giving participants sufficient opportunities to practice the MRB's (at least eighteen practice interviews). *There was no case of a library system that provided less than three days of training performing above the seventy percent average score.*
- Next in importance was participants engaging in peer coaching at least three times a week for at least four weeks after the end of the formal training.
- Also found to be an important support to continued use of the behaviors was the specific strategy of having a reference policy requiring the use of the MRB's.

The data suggest that it takes a combination of all three items to ensure good performance over time. The results were reported[13] in *Public Libraries* in 1992.

In 1994, as another long range plan for state-wide library development drew to a close, DLDS hired Transform, Inc., to conduct another unobtrusive reference survey. The median score for all library systems was seventy-five percent (complete and correct answers). The results of the 1994 survey corroborated the efficacy of the strategies mentioned above which were discovered in the 1990 study. As part of the 1994 survey, a questionnaire was devised, investigating staff perceptions of their use of the MRB's. Interestingly, no correlation was found between staff perceptions of their use of the MRB's and actual use as measured by the unobtrusive survey. This suggests that one should be cautious in using reference staff's perceptions about their performance as an indicator of actual performance.

THE MODEL REFERENCE BEHAVIORS

Over the years, the list of Model Reference Behaviors (MRB's) has changed somewhat. Most notable was the inclusion of verifying, which, after being investigated in the 1986 survey, turned out to be the most important behavior reference staff have at their disposal. Some of the behaviors identified after the 1983 survey have been dropped because their statistical correlations with good performance, although positive, are quite weak. Some other behaviors were combined or renamed, based on what was learned over time. The behaviors measured in the 1983 survey and those addressed in Transform's "Effective Reference Performance" (ERP) workshop are listed in Table 2.

The MRB's were identified because the surveys looked at, in addition to what degree reference staff provided complete and correct answers, what behaviors successful librarians used as they went about providing complete and correct answers.

The MRB's provide a structure for conducting a reference interview which allows reference staff to follow a pattern, varying behaviors depending upon the situation, which has been shown empirically to result in improved performance.

The "Effective Reference Performance" workshop is not intended to turn reference staff into robots or automatons. Specific phrases are suggested for certain situations because research has shown that these phrases are optimally efficacious. However, workshop participants are expected to modify the behaviors to fit their style of working with their customers while maintaining the basic structure of the interview.

RESEARCH ON TRAINING

If one is to conduct training, it would be helpful to know what makes training effective. Here the work[14] of Bruce Joyce, formerly of Columbia University, is revealing. Joyce and Beverly Showers, his collaborator, discovered that the effectiveness of training is directly related to the models of teaching employed. They identified four basic models of training:

1. Theory and Rationale–presenting what the skills are and why they should be used.
2. Demonstration–conducting competent modeling of the behaviors so that participants can see what the skills look like when applied.
3. Practice with Structured Feedback–providing sufficient opportunities for participants to practice using the skills and receive non-threatening feedback.
4. Peer Coaching–allowing participants to practice using the behaviors in a supportive environment and to receive technical feedback and positive reinforcement for their efforts.

TABLE 1. State-Wide Reference Survey–1983

Rank of Questions by Difficulty (11 Most Difficult)

QUESTION NUMBER	QUESTIONS LISTED BY MOST DIFFICULT TO LEAST DIFFICULT	PERCENT OF QUESTIONS ANSWERED AT LEVELS 1 OR 2	TYPE OF CONTACT PHONE IN/ WALKS IN DIRECT/ ESCALATOR	AVERAGE LENGTH OF TIME TO ANSWER QUESTION	BASIC SOURCE
29	Bks on car repair? How often change radiator coolant?	0.0	T-E	6.0 min.	Chilton's
9	Have French bks? Recipe for bouillibaisse?	5.0	W-E	5.1	Joy of Cooking
39	Bks on car repair? How often change transmission fluid?	5.0	W-E	1.7	Chilton's
38	Bks on animals? Gestation for hamsters?	18.3	W-E	4.0	World Almanac
40	Bks on dogs? Highland Terrier AKC registered?	18.3	W-E	5.3	World Almanac
6	Who said, "Victory of hope over experience"?	21.7	W	14.1	Stevenson's Home Book
8	Review of Equus as a movie?	21.7	W	8.8	Reader's Guide
26	Bks on genealogy? Address of Soc. of the Cincinnati?	23.4	T-E	6.8	World Almanac
7	Meaning of dolphin in Christian art?	26.7	W	10.0	World Book
10	Bks on WWII? Name of Tokyo Rose?	26.7	W-E	8.7	World Almanac
37	Info on Maryland? No. of delegates in MD Legislature?	26.7	W-E	3.4	World Almanac

TABLE 2. Model Reference Behaviors

CATEGORIES AND BEHAVIORS
1983 SURVEY

APPROACHABILITY
Smiles
Makes Eye Contact
Gives Friendly Verbal Greeting
Is At Same Eye Level As Patron

COMFORT
Maintains Eye Contact
Shows Relaxed Body Posture
Makes Attentive Comments
Speaks In Interested, Helpful Tone

INTEREST
Maintains Eye Contact
Is Mobile, Goes With Patron
Gives Patron Full Attention

NEGOTIATION
Asks Open Questions
Probes
Paraphrases
Clarifies
Informs
Uses Basic Sources
Goes Beyond Immediate Resources
Checks Out
Summarizes
Cites The Source

FOLLOW-UP
Asks, "Does This Completely
Answer Your Question?"
Closes The Interview Tactfully

CATEGORIES AND BEHAVIORS
ERP WORKSHOP

WELCOMING
Makes Eye Contact
Smiles
Gives Friendly Greeting

ATTENDING
Gives Full Attention
Maintains Eye Contact
Makes Attentive Comments

LISTENING
Paraphrases Or Clarifies
Does Not Interrupt

PROBING
Uses Open Probe To Initiate
Inquiry
Uses Open Probe(s) After Initial
Probe

VERIFYING
Uses Transition Phrase
Paraphrases Or Repeats Patron's
Specific Question
Asks If That Is Specific Question

SEARCHING
Accompanies Patron
Reports Progress Of Search
Offers Referral

INFORMING
Cites Source
Confirms Answer Understood

FOLLOWING UP
Asks Follow-up Question That
Addresses Specific Inquiry

Joyce and Showers discovered that when only theory and rationale were employed in workshops, the best that could be expected is that only five to ten percent of the participants would acquire the skills by the end of the workshop.

When demonstration was added to the presentation of theory and rationale, only ten to thirty percent of the participants would acquire the skills by the end of the training.

When practice with structured feedback, in a supportive, non-threatening environment, was added to the models above, then eighty to ninety percent of the participants could be expected to acquire the skills taught.

When peer coaching was added to the above models, eighty to ninety percent of the participants could be expected to acquire the skills taught.

The figures above apply to ideal conditions: highly motivated participants, expert trainers, and an excellent environment in which the training takes place (e.g., good lighting, comfortable temperature, etc.).

Before leaving this section on the acquisition of skills, more discussion on the element of structured feedback may be in order. When DLDS conducted its training in the 1980s, they taught giving feedback in what was thought to be a non-threatening way.[15] When a trainee is learning new skills, he/she is taking risks–the possibility of not doing something correctly–and is very sensitive to any feedback which might be perceived as critical or threatening. The trainers at Transform, Inc. have developed a way of giving technical feedback which improves on the original method and is perceived by participants as even less threatening. Participants are asked to come in teams of two or more from an outlet. This allows them to peer coach back on the job after the training.

The "Effective Reference Performance" workshop conducted by Transform, Inc. consists of three full days of training. During the first two days, participants are given the theory and rationale of the Model Reference Behaviors, see them demonstrated competently, and receive plenty of practice in using them in small groups. Two trainers are required for the presentation of the workshop, primarily because there are two skill areas being taught: the MRB's, and technical feedback and positive reinforcement. The trainer playing the role of the librarian needs to demonstrate the Model Reference Behaviors competently, and the trainer playing the role of the coach needs to demonstrate giving technical feedback and positive reinforcement competently. The behaviors are introduced gradually over the course of the two days, building upon previous learnings.

After the first two days, participants have a break of two to three weeks, during which time they are to go back to their work places and practice what they have learned; applying the Model Reference Behaviors in the real world with actual library customers, and coaching one another. This is a practice period during which they have an opportunity to experience successes in the application of the MRB's and to encounter problems in their application, as well as trying to put the concept of peer coaching in place.

On the third day, participants identify successes and obstacles they've encountered and are given strategies for overcoming those obstacles. In addition, they are given more practice in using the MRB's. Finally, they are given a number of strategies for transferring the behaviors permanently to the job.

TRANSFER OF TRAINING

Joyce and Showers defined effective training as not only the acquisition of skills, but also the application of those skills on the job. In investigating further they discovered that the models of training used in the workshop impacted on the application of skills on the job as well.

When only theory and rationale were presented as training models in the workshop, so that up to ten percent of the participants acquired the skills by the end of the training, after a year or so after the training, only five percent of the trainees would be applying the skills on the job.

When theory and rationale plus demonstration were presented, so that up to thirty percent of the workshop participants acquired the skills, after a year or longer, only five percent of the trainees would be using the skills on the job.

When theory and rationale, plus demonstration, plus practice with structured feedback were presented, so that up to ninety percent of the participants acquired the skills by the end of the training, only five percent of the trainees would be applying the skills on the job over time (more recent work by Michael McKibbin of California suggests that this figure might actually be closer to twenty to thirty percent in the application of the skills, and his research is persuasive).[16]

When theory and rationale, plus demonstration, plus practice with feedback, plus coaching were presented, so that up to ninety percent of the participants acquired the skills, after a year or longer, eighty to ninety percent of the trainees would be using the skills on the job.

An investigation of why, without peer coaching, workers abandoned the application of clearly useful skills in the work place revealed that the primary reason was discomfort. The new or enhanced skills interfered with their existing ways of doing things and produced discomfort. Things didn't go as well as before at first, because the new skills were not yet a habit, which produced discomfort, which caused avoidance of the new skills.

Joyce and Showers discovered an irony of effective training–trying to apply new skills makes one worse before one gets better. In trying to apply new or enhanced skills on the job, one should expect a period of "performance dip," during which time performance will get worse before, with practice, it gets better.

Peer coaching provides a support system in which another trainee provides companionship and support by providing technical feedback and positive reinforcement on behaviors done well. A new trainee will tend to concentrate on what he or she does incorrectly rather than on the many things that are done correctly. A coach helps provide perspective on the skills done well and helps the trainee get through the inevitable period of "performance dip."

SKILLS MAINTENANCE:
THE ROLE OF THE MANAGER/ADMINISTRATOR

Successful training requires not only the acquisition of skills, but also the maintenance of those skills. The "Effective Reference Performance" workshop ensures that employees acquire reference interviewing skills. The maintenance of the skills is the province of the manager.

As part of the "Effective Reference Performance" workshop, not only are workshop participants given pre-workshop readings as an assignment before attending, so that participants have a common knowledge base, but also, the immediate supervisors of attendees are given pre-workshop readings which inform them about preparing their people for attendance at the workshop and give the theory and rationale for the Model Reference Behaviors, which their staff will be learning. The supervisors also are informed about the phenomenon of "performance dip" and how they might help their staff during this phase of discomfort.

A separate, but recommended part of Transform's reference interview training consists of a one-day information session for managers of reference services. This should be attended by the managers of participants. This session provides information to help managers avoid the "Great Training Robbery."[17] Most managers are unaware of the impact of Bruce Joyce's research. If they don't choose skills training that employs those models, their training dollars are probably wasted. Transform's "Supervisors' Session" informs managers about Joyce and Shower's research, and explains peer coaching. The Model Reference Behaviors are demonstrated so that managers can recognize them when they see them. The managers are taught the importance of setting and communicating performance expectations and providing supportive feedback. They are informed about "performance dip" and given specific strategies to help their staff. They also develop an action plan that dovetails with the action plans developed by their staff in the three-day workshop.

Managers need to identify the importance of the role their agency will play in the delivery of reference services. This role should be clearly stated in policies, procedures, and guidelines. In order to do their jobs better, employees need to know what to do, how well to do it, and how well they are doing it.

Training in the Model Reference Behaviors can provide staff with the knowledge of what they are to do and how to do it. By the end of the "Effective Reference Performance" workshop, staff know what specific behaviors they are supposed to do and they demonstrate that they can do them. The workshop provides the skills so that staff know what to do.

In addition, staff need to know how well they are expected to do their jobs. Good managers communicate with their staff what their expectations of reference service performance are. After hearing the responses of hundreds of managers who have attended the "Supervisors' Session," it is clear that most managers or administrators have never addressed this problem.

Also, staff need to know how well they are doing their jobs. This demands feedback from their managers. Transform's studies of managers' use of good management behaviors showed that most managers and administrators lack the skills of setting performance expectations, and giving supportive feedback. Comparison of managers' perceptions of their use of effective management behaviors and their staffs' perceptions of the managers' use of the behaviors reveals a significant discrepancy. Most managers think that they employ good management behaviors, but studies belie this belief. This should not be an unexpected phenomenon given that most managers and administrators have been "elevated" to those positions without ever being given training on how to deal effectively with employees face-to-face. As a result of studies in this area, Transform, Inc. developed a two-day training session, "Effective Management Performance," with half-day options, to teach the skills that were found to be lacking.

Being supportive of newly trained staff requires support for the coaching process. Managers need to recognize the behaviors the staff have been trained to use, and they need to reinforce the use of these specific behaviors when they see or hear them. Specific, descriptive praise for the new skills is most effective when delivered at the time of the observation.

IN CONCLUSION

For years emphasis in reference training has focused on the tools where the answer can be found. Tools training is important, but it is not particularly useful if the librarian does not know the actual nature of the patron's question.

Studies have shown that patrons want answers to their questions and that the public library is an effective place to obtain them. Interview skills training for reference staff is critical to helping librarians determine the patron's information need. The use of the Model Reference Behaviors has been shown to directly affect the interview process and the accuracy of reference performance.

To be effective, reference interview skills training needs to focus on the MRB's, to include sufficient practice, and to incorporate peer coaching, as in-workshop and transfer techniques.

The role of the manager is critical to letting reference staff know what to do, how well they are to do it, and how well it is being done. Offering staff training in the reference interview skills requires managers to do their homework before sending their staff to training.

As managers may have already suspected, effective reference service requires more than one initially expects–more than what initially meets the eye–when a library advertises that it offers reference service.

NOTES

1. Lebby, D. Edwin. Information Needs of the People of the Eastern Shore. Annapolis Research Corp., 1976 (ED 134191). This in-person household survey (approximately 30 minutes in length) was conducted in 8 counties on the Eastern Shore of Maryland and had 1280 respondents.

2. Westat, Inc. The Library and Information Needs of Southern Maryland Residents. Westat, Inc., 1975 (ED 119679). This in-person household survey (approximately 45 minutes in length) was conducted in 3 counties of Southern Maryland and had 756 respondents.

3. Gers, Ralph. "Up Yours: How To Improve Your Library's Performance At Minimum Cost." Paper presented at the Public Library Association National Conference, Baltimore, 1983.

4. Gers, Ralph, and Seward, Lillie. "Improving Reference Performance: Results of a Statewide Study." Library Journal (November 1, 1995): 32-25.

5. Crowley, Terence. "Half-Right Reference: Is It True?" RQ (Fall 1985): 59-68.

6. Hernon, Peter, and McClure, Charles R. "Unobtrusive Testing: The 55 Percent Rule." Library Journal (April 15,1986): 37-41.

7. Childers, Thomas. The Effectiveness of Information Service In Public Libraries: Suffolk County; Final Report. Philadelphia: Drexel University, 1978.

8. Sass, Rivkah. "Hey Kid! Did You Get An Answer To Your Question?" Paper presented at the American Library Association National Conference, San Francisco, 1997.

9. Hernon and McClure, op. cit., 41.

10. Crowley, op. cit., 59.

11. Seward, Lillie et al. "Users Deserve Better Than a 50/50 Chance: Improving Reference Performance." Paper presented at the Public Library Association National Conference, St. Louis, 1986.

12. Gers, Ralph et al. "The 77 Percent Solution; A Formula For Improving Reference Performance." Paper presented at the Public Library Association National Conference, Pittsburgh, 1988.

13. Dyson, Lillie Seward. "Improving Reference Services: A Maryland Training Program Brings Positive Results." Public Libraries (Sept. /Oct. 1992): 284-289.

14. Joyce, Bruce R., and Showers, Beverly. Power In Staff Development Through Research On Training. Alexandria, VA: Association for Supervision and Curriculum Development, 1983. (ED 240667).

15. Gers, Ralph, and Seward, Lillie. "'I Heard You Say, . . . ' Peer Coaching for More Effective Reference Service." *In Information Brokers and Reference Services*, edited by Robin Kinder and Bill Katz. New York: The Haworth Press, Inc., 1988.

16. McKibbin, Michael. "Teacher Training That Makes A Difference," Seminar presented at the Maryland State Department of Education, August 26, 1985.

17. Zenger, Jack. "The Great Training Robbery." Training and Development Journal (December, 1980): 36-49.

Technology Training
at the St. Louis Public Library

Barbara Knotts

SUMMARY. The St. Louis Public Library's (SLPL) technology training programs for staff and public are visible ways for the library to accomplish its mission and goals. SLPL's official mission is to "provide learning resources and information services that support and *improve* (the author's emphasis) individual, family, and community life." This mission, along with the two institutional goals to "promote public use of modern information technology" and "ensure that the library's resources are available to all," set the framework for these programs (statement adopted by SLPL Board of Directors, January, 1994).

The library's training programs are continually evolving to meet the changes in technology, products, and services used by staff and provided to the public. Grants from the State of Missouri, MCI, Department of Education, Microsoft, and Gates Library Foundation, along with local tax-supported revenues, enable the library to continue expansion of its training facilities and programs.

The library constantly evaluates its training programs. We learn from each of them, applying that knowledge to make all programs stronger and more useful. The result is that staff and the public can effectively use technology to get access to information affecting their daily lives.

To fully understand SLPL's commitment to training and its determination to be a leader in this area, it is necessary to look at our community and our library system. *[Article copies available for a fee from The Haworth Document Delivery Service: 1-800-342-9678. E-mail address: getinfo@ haworthpressinc.com <Website: http://www.haworthpressinc.com>]*

Barbara Knotts is Manager of Electronic Collections, St. Louis Public Library.

[Haworth co-indexing entry note]: "Technology Training at the St. Louis Public Library." Knotts, Barbara. Co-published simultaneously in *Journal of Library Administration* (The Haworth Information Press, an imprint of The Haworth Press, Inc.) Vol. 29, No. 1, 1999, pp. 17-35; and: *Library Training for Staff and Customers* (ed: Sara Ramser Beck) The Haworth Information Press, an imprint of The Haworth Press, Inc., 2000, pp. 17-35. Single or multiple copies of this article are available for a fee from The Haworth Document Delivery Service [1-800-342-9678, 9:00 a.m. - 5:00 p.m. (EST). E-mail address: getinfo@haworthpressinc.com].

17

KEYWORDS. Staff training, training of employees, technology training, customer service, customer training

THE ST. LOUIS COMMUNITY

The St. Louis Public Library (SLPL) District is located in the city of
St. Louis and serves an urban population of 396,685. The library
provides materials and services to several distinct, diverse constituen-
cies. The primary constituency served is the taxpayers and residents of
the city. The library also functions as a research center for the more
than 200,000 commuters who live outside the city but work within the
city. It serves the State of Missouri as a major urban resource center
under agreement with the State Library. Increasingly each of these
groups is expecting SLPL to provide electronic services and training
ranging from basic introductions to advanced concepts.

The population of the city is racially diverse, with approximately
45% of the population listed as African-American, 51% Caucasian,
and 4% "other," principally Hispanic and Asian. Overall this population falls below the national average in family income and educational
level. And, in spite of the national economic upsurge through the
1980s, poverty has increased in St. Louis.

Access to computers is limited in St. Louis. SLPL survey data
indicates one in four city homes have a computer. That goes to less
than 1 in 10 in our poorer neighborhoods. And in St. Louis with a high
poverty level, there are many such neighborhoods.

This situation is made worse by lack of access to public computers.
City public schools and most parochial schools still lack even a single
computer in many classrooms. Most schools in St. Louis do not offer
electronic media access either to the general community or to students
after-school or on the weekends.

Recent SLPL focus-groups testify to the need to provide access to
computers and training on how to use them effectively to users of all
ages. The library had groups of teens, working-age adults, and seniors
that revealed a high demand for computer access and training. These
groups indicated that as many as 50% of all St. Louisians have come to
expect that their library system become a principal provider of computer
training. We are expected to be the community's "computer teacher."

THE ST. LOUIS PUBLIC LIBRARY SYSTEM

Innovative leadership, talented staff, good financial position, positive reputation within the community and a solid technology plan are some of the elements that put the St. Louis Public Library system in a position to meet many of the community's expectations related to technology training.

Currently the library system consists of a central library plus 15 branch locations of various sizes located in neighborhoods throughout the city. The staff numbers approximately 250 (FTE's) including 15 staff dedicated to system-wide technology maintenance and training. SLPL currently operates more than 450 PCs distributed throughout the system. These machines serve both the public and the staff in carrying out daily activities.

A successful tax campaign in 1994 helped increase revenues. As a result, about three years ago, SLPL undertook a 10-year Capital Improvement Plan. Under this plan each location, from the smallest to the largest, has or will undergo renovation, expansion, or replacement. Already in the last three years locations have received major upgrades to their equipment, introduction of Internet access, capacity to house and access all types of technology, and the opening of Neighborhood Computing Centers.

Recent grants from the Microsoft Corporation and Gates Library Foundation have supplemented library funding for computer resources at the Neighborhood Computing Centers. Each of these state-of-the-art centers features PCs for public use and a variety of educational and recreational software packages. Since 1996 the library has opened four of these centers with four more scheduled to open during 1999.

Networked public access PCs with stand-alone CD-ROM and WAN products are available at all SLPL locations in both the adult and juvenile areas. These public access computers are divided into four categories: Authorship/Educational Software, Internet, Reference, and Catalog. Software titles are chosen to reflect the needs of each location's public users. Usage of the Authorship/Education Software and Internet machines requires a valid library card and can be scheduled with some time restrictions being applied. Networked reference products are available at each location for use by staff and public. The Reference and Catalog public access machines are not scheduled, being available on a walk-up, first-come basis with no library card required.

All SLPL locations, except the two mini-branches, currently have public access to the Internet with the number of PCs dedicated to this function ranging from two (one adult and one juvenile) at several locations to 10 (including adult and juvenile) at another location. In December, 1998 and January, 1999 additional Internet PCs were added at several locations to meet growing public demand.

Staff have also benefited from changes in technology. Currently managers at all of SLPL's locations have their own PCs with word processing, e-mail, scheduling, and Internet access. All staff, not just managers, have e-mail accounts and access to the "First Search" and "EBSCOHost" electronic products. These administrative PCs and products enhance organizational effectiveness and overall communications.

In February, 1998 SLPL contracted with Data Research Associates (DRA) to provide the library with a new automation system. A crucial aspect of the migration from the current in-house system to the DRA product was the library administration's priority that quality training be provided for both staff and public.

With this background, it is not surprising that the library's Board of Directors and Administration make access to computers and the training to use them effectively a top priority for both staff and public. The commitment includes the financial resources necessary to increase the system's network structure, add hardware and software, train staff and provide technical support.

STAFF TRAINING

SLPL's commitment to technology includes its support for quality staff training. Library Administration and the Board of Directors recognized that if the technology being placed throughout the system was to be used effectively and staff qualified to provide public service, staff technology training programs needed to be established.

As a first step, Administration and the Board of Directors, with staff input, wrote or modified policies and procedures related to electronic resources. Staff now had documents they could reference when questions were asked about use of the Internet or other public access computers, and appropriate patron behavior. These documents continue to be used in staff training sessions. To help both staff and the public these documents also appear on the SLPL Website (http://www.slpl.lib.mo.us).

Under the direction of the Administration, the Technology Services Department assumed responsibility for staff technology training. A new position, now called Manager of Electronic Collections, was created within the Technology Services Department. As that manager, I was given the responsibility to provide training and retraining for staff at all levels and locations. Later my responsibilities increased to include public training and a position called Training Specialist, reporting to me, was added.

As I began this position, funds were allocated for a staff training lab. The lab included eight PC workstations and an instructor's station with the ability to project to a wall-mounted screen. Several software packages, including word processing and an Internet browser, were installed on all PCs. I now had a well-equipped lab to hold group training sessions, plus a place for staff to practice in one-on-one situations. The lab could also be used to evaluate new electronic products.

After getting input from staff about types of training they needed, two Technology Services staff and I began to plan one-on-one and group sessions. This was the time several locations began getting computers for the public to use and managers began receiving their administrative PCs. Staff needed training on how to use the machines and software on them. We provided this training in two-hour sessions at their locations. Sessions covered an introduction to the use of the PC, discussion of security, and hands-on opportunities to use the software.

One of the first system-wide staff training programs I set up was a class, "Introduction to the Internet." Before any public access Internet PCs were installed, SLPL wanted staff to have basic knowledge about the Internet and understand SLPL's policies and procedures. Hands-on sessions, open to all staff with the approval of their managers, were held. Over 200 staff took advantage of this opportunity. To enable staff to keep up with changes, periodic Webtrekkers classes are held covering subjects such as "Beyond the Basics," "Kids on the Web," and "Finding Government Information." SLPL staff from throughout the system contributed to the success of the Webtrekker classes by volunteering to be presenters. The introductory course is repeated twice a year for new staff or staff that want a refresher.

Other system-wide training courses are conducted as new electronic products are made available to staff. Several sessions about using

OCLC's "FirstSearch" product and EBSCO's magazine index, "EB-SCOHost," have been provided with staff from all locations attending. Staff are able to use the skills gained in these sessions to provide their patrons with access to new information sources. Managers at SLPL's smaller locations tell me this access, and their ability to use it effectively, allow them to provide a new level of public service.

Several important lessons were learned in these initial training sessions that we have applied to all subsequent sessions. The important ones are:

- *Customize the presentation.*
- *Provide meaningful handouts* to help with practice after the training sessions.
- *Schedule sessions* when those attending will not be called away to perform other duties.
- *Share and communicate.* As a representative of Technology Services I could listen to issues and concerns of the staff and relay that information to my supervisor, the Director of Technology Services. That information could be used to aid future technology planning.

Since 1996 SLPL has renovated four locations, reopening them with networked administrative PCs for the staff and the Neighborhood Computer Centers discussed above for the public. It was vital that staff feel comfortable with the new hardware and software. So, in the weeks before the locations reopened, staff were given the opportunity to train using the equipment and software that would be at their location. Sessions were led by the Training Specialist, other members of the Technology Services Department and myself. These sessions gave all staff an introduction to using the equipment, general troubleshooting suggestions, and time to work with the software products. Some of the sessions were held at the Central Library lab. Other sessions were held at the location. Staff said both were helpful. The sessions at the lab allowed staff to concentrate on specific products, while those at their location helped them understand how the equipment would work within their daily activities.

Not all technology training at SLPL takes place in a classroom setting. E-mail is another good training tool. Each week I use e-mail to distribute a list of "Interesting Links" to staff. Most of them are submitted by staff members alerting other staff to Websites to use in their daily activities. These sites also become a part of the Premier Internet Resources section of SLPL's Website and reach out to the community. This has proven to be a good way to let staff share good resources with other staff and continually upgrade the Website.

Staff training took on a new dimension in February, 1998. At that time SLPL selected Data Research Associates (DRA) to provide the library with a new automation system. Between then and December 30, 1998 when SLPL began to use the new system, training efforts focused on the staff. This article is being written in January, 1999 and efforts to support staff continue as we work with the new system.

When Dr. Glen Holt, SLPL's Executive Director, announced the DRA/SLPL contract, he appointed an Implementation Committee. The Committee's charge included the goal of ensuring staff receive quality training and be given the opportunity to become comfortable with the new system before we began to use it. As Chair of the DRA Implementation Committee, this became one of my top priorities. The Committee devised a training plan, much of which has been successfully implemented. In this plan DRA supplied training to eight SLPL staff members for each module (Circulation, OPAC, Technical Services, Acquisitions, Serials, and Operations). Each training team was then responsible for providing training to other staff. A facilitator was selected for each team to ensure coordination and consistency in the sessions. As this article is being written the Library's OPAC and Circulation teams have each completed initial and refresher training for over 160 staff members.

As the DRA implementation project continues we modify our training plan to reflect lessons learned during our recent experiences. These include:

- *Teams Work.* The team approach is working well. The eight members on OPAC and Circulation teams met the day after they completed their DRA-supplied training. At that time each team divided into four groups of two trainers. Each of these four groups is then responsible for 2-3 training sessions. The team as a whole agreed on an outline for each session and the handouts that should be used. The goal is to ensure quality training at all sessions, with staff receiving the same information.
- *Managers First.* The first session for each module is for managers, followed by sessions for other staff. This gives managers the opportunity to learn about the system first and become the con-

tact person at each location. All staff questions are to be funneled through the managers to the DRA Implementation Committee.

- *Handouts Make a Difference.* The training teams create handouts to be used during the training sessions and later for reference as staff practice at their locations. DRA supplied the training handouts to the library in electronic format. The teams took these handouts and customized them to SLPL. Teams have received more positive comments about the importance of the handouts than any other aspect of the training.

- *Content Should Vary.* The DRA Implementation Committee's Training Plan includes in-depth training for staff who will use a particular module on a daily basis, demonstrations for staff who use it less regularly, and planned refresher courses just before we begin to use the system. We believe this approach makes more effective use of staff resources and ensures organization-wide understanding of the new system.

- *Let Them Practice.* The best training will be forgotten if staff do not have the opportunity to practice their skills. Equipment was available at all locations that enabled staff to practice new skills after the training sessions. Managers worked with their staff to assure that time to practice is scheduled. A checklist of procedures staff should be able to perform was given to each manager to aid them as they worked with their staff.

- *Provide Opportunities for Refresher Training.* Staff refresher OPAC and Circulation sessions were scheduled at various times and locations during the two weeks before SLPL began using the new system. Each session included a review of topics covered in the initial training sessions, updates on procedural changes, plus the opportunity to practice.

- *Training Doesn't Stop When the New System Begins.* The DRA Implementation Committee, along with SLPL administration, knew that no matter how comprehensive the staff training activities were or how much staff practice occurred, there would be unanswered questions and needs when we began to use the new system. To help, several measures were undertaken:

  - *HelpDesk Expanded.* For the first two weeks after the new automation system was implemented, the Technology Services Department made sure the HelpDesk was available during all hours that any library location was open. Staff could contact the HelpDesk either via the telephone or a special e-mail account. We used the staff newsletter and memos to managers to be sure everyone was aware the HelpDesk was the place to find answers. All requests were logged and monitored by Technology Services' Manager of User Support to assure the quality and timely response of answers to staff.

Temporary help was hired to answer phones for the first two weeks after the library began to use the new system. The Training Specialist and I had the temporary help begin two days before SLPL began to use the new system. We used those two days to provide training sessions about the new automation system. Our goal was not to teach the temporary employees all the specifics about the new system. Rather, we wanted to make them comfortable with the system's framework and introduce them to the vocabulary that staff would use when logging a question. Permanent Technology Services' staff also attended these sessions. The results were very positive. The temporary staff worked effectively with permanent staff. Because of the training, the temporary staff were able to get details for the logs that minimized the need for permanent staff to do multiple call-backs, identify concerns that were being logged by several locations, and answer some general questions.

- *Extra Staff Support.* Members of the DRA Implementation Committee, staff trainers, and other managers rotated throughout the locations during the first few days after we began to use the new system. These staff could often answer staff questions, review content with staff from their training sessions, and do initial troubleshooting.
- *Continued Communication.* Based on a review of questions sent to the HelpDesk and those asked of our rotating staff, we were able to identify training issues that needed follow-up. The weekly staff newsletter and e-mail again proved to be excellent communication tools. FAQs were distributed, giving staff ideas on using the system more effectively and keeping them up to date on changes. At a supervisor's meeting held about two weeks after initial system implementation I gave a project update and moderated a question and answer period. I

used this opportunity as a mini-training session, clarifying several procedures.

Staff training for the new system was a success. When the doors opened the morning of December 30, 1998 staff stepped up to their PCs and provided the quality service the St. Louis community expects. That is not to say that there were not questions. But the questions were generally not about topics covered in depth during the training sessions and reviewed by staff during their practice. Instead, they tended to be about more complex functions or specifics of conversion data. Follow-up training sessions will address these issues.

Staff technology training, whether it is for new software products, the Internet, or a new automation system, is an ongoing process. This process must balance the changing needs of staff with available resources. This is particularly true for SLPL with its rapidly changing technology environment and dedication to software innovation. SLPL's growth in staff training programs in the last four years has resulted in a staff more confident in their skills and knowledge. New tools and staff resources continue to be made available. With staff training programs in place and continuing to be enhanced, SLPL could begin to respond to the community's requests for public technology training programs.

PUBLIC TRAINING

SLPL's first response for technology training for the public came in 1997 when the library began offering courses on using the Internet. Knowing from focus groups that such training would be in high demand but that staff resources were limited, SLPL placed a small article in the library newsletter announcing a course on the Internet for adults and one for juveniles. People could register by calling the Marketing Department's answering machine. Response was so overwhelming that the original plan to provide two sessions quickly expanded into four sessions. Within a few days, SLPL had to post a message saying that all spots were filled.

Staff from the Technology Services Department called registrants back in the order of phone calls received, allowing them to pick the session they would attend. A waiting list was kept that had enough people to run several additional sessions. The waiting list, plus word of mouth, made further advertising in 1997 unnecessary.

The Internet classes proved to be very popular with members of the St. Louis community. Following the same format, both sessions geared to adults and juveniles included an overview of the Internet, instruction on using a browser to visit Websites, techniques for utilizing a search engine, and tips for being safe and savvy on the Web. The classes ran about two hours, but usually lasted longer. Attendees got so involved they did not want to leave.

The Internet classes gave SLPL a good opportunity to find what worked, and what did not, when providing training for the public.

- *RSVPs Help.* To insure that attendees had access to machines, pre-registration was required. Because the classes were so popular, they quickly filled up and people had to be turned away. But most classes had a percentage of people who did not show up. To help minimize this reminder calls were placed a few days before the classes. As the number of classes increased, staff resources we not always available to do this but SLPL volunteers continue to do this often as possible.
- *Find a Partner.* We found partnering a good way to increase the effectiveness of training. SLPL and OASIS (senior citizens) worked together to present several Internet sessions for seniors. A good partner can help with publicity along with giving you ideas for customized handouts and successful presentation techniques.
- *Use Technology to Train Technology.* The most successful classes were those that mixed hands-on experiences with demonstrations. With adult attendees it was very important to quickly get to hands-on exercises. SLPL accomplished this by having the classes in computing centers or labs where enough PCs were available. We found many of the people that attended the classes did not know how to use the mouse and had limited keyboarding skills. Several ways were tried to make keyboarding easier including putting two people at a PC, providing a mini-class just before the training session that covered keyboarding and mouse basics, slowing the mouse speed down, and making other input devices such as the Easyball available.
- *Make the Training Personal.* SLPL found it very useful to have multiple training staff or representatives of the partners at each session. The extra staff could work more one-on-one with attendees having difficulties, thus keeping the class moving at an even

pace. The staff member who works closely with the SLPL Web-site helped me with many of these sessions. As both a parent and avid Internet user, her experiences greatly enriched the sessions. At the same time, she got ideas from the classes that we incorporated into the Website. Plenty of opportunities were also allowed for attendees to share their experiences. That helped the instructor (me) find out what each attendee was really looking for and to better customize the class. I kept asking questions of the attendees to be sure they were understanding the concepts. Their answers helped me to know when to slow down or go back and review. It also reminded me to use language they understood, not jargon related to computers or libraries.

- *If You Enjoy It, They Will.* It probably goes without saying, but I believe it is important for the instructors to enjoy what they are doing. And that enjoyment must communicate itself to the audience. When you break down the barriers between the instructors and audience, everyone is more comfortable. We found being in the room before the sessions began and greeting everyone paid big dividends. We used the opportunity to get conversations going, tell light-hearted stories about ourselves, and show the audience how excited we were about the session. It gave the audience members some opportunities to share their experience and expectations.

- *Don't Be Fooled by Good Reviews.* Evaluations were used at all training sessions and reviewed thoroughly after each session. We responded to new needs by modifying the classes based on suggestions we received. Most evaluations were positive but I wondered if the responses would be so positive if attendees were asked several weeks later. To answer this question, a Technology Services staff member and I ran a telephone survey about three weeks after one session. All attendees still praised the class. But only about half had actually used the Internet after the class. Access was still the big problem, reinforcing for SLPL the need to increase the number of PCs throughout the city and publicize their availability.

Most evaluations included the request that SLPL offer more, and a wider variety, of computer classes. It became apparent even with help from other staff and partners, I could not meet this demand. In response, SLPL Administration created a new full-time Trainer Specialist position, reporting to me. This staff member's responsibilities include conducting technology-related training sessions for staff and public. He is also responsible for coordinating training activities and evaluating them. He creates a training calendar that is distributed monthly listing all staff and public training activities for the next several months.

While the Trainer Specialist and I could now provide more staff and public training activities, growing demands by both groups showed us we needed to formulate a more systematic approach to training. Grants from MCI and the U.S. Department of Education gave us the means to do this.

NetLINK was the first computer training program set up. Its goal is to provide public technology training that is high quality, economical and makes the best use of staff resources. The program is a result of a grant from MCI's LibraryLINK community service initiative. Through it, SLPL has the opportunity to provide our public with a wide range of free training sessions on everything from basic computer use to advanced Internet searching. Much of the coordination responsibility for this program is handled by the Trainer Specialist.

Using funds from the MCI LibraryLINK, SLPL contracted with public–and private–sector computer instruction providers to develop instructional materials and for these providers to give actual sessions based on those materials. Currently SLPL works with three such providers who present the following classes multiple times each month: Introduction to the Internet (for Adults and Juveniles), Word (Basic and Intermediate), Excel (Basic and Intermediate), ABCs of Computers, and Basic Windows. Between thirty and forty sessions are held monthly.

As part of the contract with each of these providers, all curriculum materials and handouts are the property of SLPL. These curriculum materials can be used repeatedly at a low cost. SLPL staff can use these to present sessions when the providers are not available and after the MCI LibraryLINK project is completed.

SLPL's experience working with the providers continues to be a learning process. We have discovered the following:

- *Multiple Providers Is a Plus.* The library prepared a Request for Proposal (RFP) that was distributed by the library's Materials Management Department. The successful bidders were chosen based on criteria in the RFP, using procedures set by the Materials Management Department. The RFP contained a Scope of Work section that outlined the project and included language that would allow the library to contract with multiple vendors for a particular time period that could be expanded. That gave the library the opportunity to extend the project beyond the initial grant funding. The library chose to look for multiple vendors so that the quality of presentations could be compared, classes could continue if one provider chose not to continue after the initial period, and the number and content of the classes could easily be increased.

- *Quality Control Is a Must.* After the providers were chosen, SLPL staff decided the classes each provider would present. Several meetings were held with each provider to agree on the curriculum and schedule. It was mandatory that providers customize the curriculum to reflect the needs of the SLPL audiences. After the curriculum materials were prepared by the provider and approved by SLPL, the first classes were scheduled. The Training Specialist or I attended the first few sessions presented by each provider to assure the quality of the presenter and content covered. Library staff receive the evaluations for each class and review them closely.

- *Choose the Courses Carefully.* Scheduling is done by SLPL staff. An attempt is made to balance the courses with the needs of the community, hours the training facilities are available, and availability of the instructor. We found it good to schedule basic classes the first few months. We continue to repeat these courses, but now that community members have taken them, the more advanced courses have an audience. It is important to schedule the classes at various times. Not everyone who wants a class on word processing can come during the evening or on the weekends.

- *Don't Forget Your Staff.* We expect to add additional classes in the future. Some will team the provider's staff with SLPL staff. Others will likely involve SLPL staff using the provider's curriculums as a framework for the classes. And still others will be prepared and taught by staff from Technology Services and other SLPL departments. Content of these courses comes from suggestions submitted by staff and received as part of the current course evaluations. Courses being considered are "Lunch Box Internet

Sessions" that will cover subject-specific Websites, College/Financial Aid resources, and Family Computing.

- *Schedule System-Wide; Register Locally.* The Training Specialist is responsible for distributing a system-wide training calendar during the last week of each month for classes scheduled for the next month. The calendar includes a date and time for registration. No registrations are taken before that time. Members of the public that want to sign up for the courses must contact the location where the class will be held. SLPL found that was the fairest way to fill the courses without overbooking. Usually most classes are filled within the first few days. The average class size increased almost 30% between the first and second month they were offered.
- *Plan for Instructor No-Shows.* Communication between SLPL and the providers is crucial. During the first few months, several times the provider's trainer did not show up at the correct time or location. Some, but not all, of that was due to miscommunication. SLPL is adding an amendment to the contract to reinforce the provider's responsibility for instructors to meet their commitments. SLPL created a procedure for staff at the training locations to follow if the trainer does not show up. SLPL staff contact each provider weekly to review the training commitments for that week.

The Training Specialist and I continue to create and present sessions to supplement those covered by the MCI grant. As new locations open we present sessions related to library topics. Two classes that are always filled are "Connect at the Library," a walk-through at the new location that includes an explanation of the new electronic resources (Internet, Authorship/Education, and Reference computers) and "Search the Catalog," an introduction to using the library's catalog that includes brief instructions about using Windows and the mouse.

In addition to SLPL's NetLINK and Technology Services staff classroom training activities, one-on-one training programs have expanded in the last three years. As the number of public access PCs and variety of software products increases throughout the library system, so does the demand by the community for guidance to use them. The library responded with three programs of interest.

- *Library Technicians Project.* In June, 1998 SLPL began its Library Technician (Technology) program. Four staff members were hired with their primary responsibility being to assist patrons with existing technology in one-on-one situations throughout the system. This assistance includes answering questions about the use of various equipment and software. They are assigned to multiple locations at times when that location has the most need, usually after school, in the evening, and on Saturdays. The presence of these technicians provides an added degree of public service for library patrons. Library technicians are hired based on their ability to work effectively with the public, understanding of technology, and positive attitude.

I choose staff for these positions based on my belief that an understanding of technology and software is a plus, but the ability to provide quality customer service is a must. This position calls for the technicians to work effectively with people of all ages and needs. They must balance multiple, simultaneous demands for attention and always continue to be courteous. They must be prepared to get a patron started for the first time on the Internet and then turn around and answer a complex question about using Excel. It is therefore important to hire the right people.

It is also important to provide them with the right kind of training before assigning the technicians to locations. At SLPL the Training Specialist and I put together training modules based on small tasks that are immediately cumulative. These modules include public service skills, general library operations, communications, troubleshooting, setup, hardware/software products, and security. Technicians are trained and certified in these areas before they are assigned. Weekly training meetings are held with the library technicians as a group to discuss issues and foster a team feeling.

The response to this program has been so positive that we are currently increasing the number of technicians. Each library technician now averages over 100 questions answered per week. Library technicians do not replace other staff's responsibility to understand technology. In fact, one of the many outcomes of this program has been that the library technicians share information and knowledge about technology with both the staff and public. This is increasingly important as SLPL patrons expect staff to understand software products and the Internet in-depth and as SLPL provides more public access computers at its locations.

- *Project REAL.* In October, 1997 SLPL received a two-year grant from the U.S. Department of Education to implement its Project REAL (Reading And Learning) program, a library-based community outreach program designed to improve reading skills among children ages 3-8. As part of this program I worked with other library staff to provide teen volunteers, called Homework Helpers, training on the use of technology available to the public and the policies and procedures that relate to them. These teens then work one-on-one with the children showing them how products on the computers can help with homework assignments and free-time activities. As another part of this grant, the families of these children were invited to two sessions at the library. I took that opportunity to introduce them to the variety of resources available on the Internet and how parents and children could use the library's computers to share this information.
- *Volunteers.* SLPL is beginning to assign volunteers to help with technology. While not expected to have the same level of expertise as the library technicians, these volunteers are very important as they supplement other available staff at busy locations. This program is just beginning, but already I have provided training sessions for volunteers covering a general overview of technology, policies, security, and printing. The Training Specialist trained about 20 volunteers to use the new OPACs. These volunteers now work one-on-one with the public at several locations. Standardized training for volunteers increases the probability that quality service will be provided in a consistent manner.

In spite of the number of staff being made available throughout the system to help the public with technology and the increased knowledge of all the staff, demands are often greater than the Library can meet. To help with this, SLPL is creating one-page sheets of information for each software product on the public access computers. The sheet will include instructions for getting into the product, using the product's Help utility, printing, exiting the product, and a list of known shortcuts. Each public access computer will have a folder attached to it containing a sheet for all products on that machine.

FUTURE TRAINING PLANS

In the last few years, SLPL's technology training programs have grown and changed to meet staff and public needs. The library must continue to maintain these programs and take advantage of changes in available technology as we plan for future training opportunities.

- *New DRA System.* Currently SLPL is planning training opportunities to introduce our community to the new DRA system. We will use the information gained from our training sessions at the opening of our newly renovated branches. That includes keeping the sessions short and to the point, making them relevant to each audience, providing both classroom and one-on-one training opportunities, distributing handouts, and scheduling the sessions at various times on days throughout the week.
- *More Public Computer Training.* A second project in the planning stage is that of enlarging the number and content of our technology training sessions. The library recently received a grant from the State of Missouri that will allow us to continue to provide training for the public. By mid-1999 at least two of the smaller new Neighborhood Computing Centers and the large new lab at our central library will provide us with additional training facilities. Using information gained from staff suggestions and evaluations provided by community members who attended current sessions, new classes are being set up. We hope to respond to the need for more advanced software product classes, family computing evenings, constructing personal homepages, and subject-specific Internet classes for adults and juveniles. Staff from our central library are working on a series of Internet LunchBox specials at which staff members will talk about favorite Websites on a particular subject and provide handouts.

SLPL is also looking at using technology in new, innovative ways.

- *Website.* We expect to develop the interactive nature of the library's Website and provide training resources to enable the public to use these enhancements. I see opportunities for public training on specific software products as they become available on the SLPL public access computers. These Web-based tutorials could be available to the public at times convenient for them from their homes, schools, businesses.

- *Intranet.* Plans are also underway for the creation of the library's Intranet, the internal Website for staff. When implemented it will provide staff with standard, system-wide access to policies, procedures, reference tools, interactive training exercises, training calendars, and much more. I can see how video and audio technology could be used to enhance training opportunities. Hardware distributed throughout the system will ensure all staff have access to these resources. On the one hand it will mean staff training programs must be formulated. But, it also will provide an avenue for staff training and performance appraisal. I believe the Intranet will a major training tool for the next several years.
- *Training Facility Use by Outside Groups.* School, business, and community groups are starting to ask the library to provide training staff to customize classes for their members and present them in SLPL's computer labs. Others want to use the training facilities, but provide their own trainers. Several of the groups would use software currently on the PCs in the training facility; other groups want to load additional products. These requests raise community, staff, and technology, fee, and security issues. SLPL's Board and Administration will formulate policy to address these requests.

Technology will continue to be used at the St. Louis Public Library to enrich and add service options. Our technology training programs for staff and the public must be ready to meet the new challenges and opportunities that will result. We must identify mechanisms to allow measurement of the effectiveness of these programs.

Using past experiences along with new, innovative ideas, SLPL will meet these objectives as it continues to be a leader and fulfill its mission to "provide learning resources and information services that support and improve individual, family, and community life."

Training Staff for Business Reference

Craig Wilkins

SUMMARY. Effective training for reference staff working with business reference subjects should be an ongoing focus for administrators concerned with providing quality service to patrons and meeting the needs of staff. Learning business reference shares some passing similarities with learning a foreign language and can produce anxiety in staff new to the field. Successful training programs create opportunities for staff to learn based on a process of realization and familiarity. Characteristics of information-seeking behavior by patrons with business subjects are discussed. Exercises and training aids are described including methods of measurement and affirmation. *[Article copies available for a fee from The Haworth Document Delivery Service: 1-800-342-9678. E-mail address: getinfo@haworthpressinc.com <Website: http://www.haworthpressinc.com>]*

KEYWORDS. Training and development, reference services, business reference

Learning business reference is similar to learning a foreign language. The reference librarian fresh to the subject is suddenly thrust into a world where new vocabulary words and reference tools with peculiar indexes predominate. There are elements of "culture shock"

Craig Wilkins is Head of the Business and Science Department of the Orange County Library System in Orlando, FL. He earned his MLS from Florida State University and is a member of the American Library Association, where he has been active in the Business Reference and Adult Services Section of RUSA for a number of years.

[Haworth co-indexing entry note]: "Training Staff for Business Reference." Wilkins, Craig. Co-published simultaneously in *Journal of Library Administration* (The Haworth Information Press, an imprint of The Haworth Press, Inc.) Vol. 29, No. 1, 1999, pp. 37-45; and: *Library Training for Staff and Customers* (ed: Sara Ramser Beck) The Haworth Information Press, an imprint of The Haworth Press, Inc., 2000, pp. 37-45. Single or multiple copies of this article are available for a fee from The Haworth Document Delivery Service [1-800-342-9678, 9:00 a.m. - 5:00 p.m. (EST). E-mail address: getinfo@haworthpressinc.com].

as they learn to deal with the new clientele. Unsettled feelings arise and are compounded by the fact that most librarians come from liberal arts backgrounds with little prior exposure to business fields. And all of this is cast against a background of steady demand. Business-oriented reference questions, particularly in public libraries, can occupy a third or more of the reference staff's attention.

Effective training for reference staff working in this subject matter should be an ongoing focus for administrators concerned with providing quality service to patrons and meeting the needs of staff. "Efficient librarians are made not born."[1] A solid training program aimed at teaching staff the "foreign" language of business reference and overcoming the anxiety of working in the field is a key ingredient in providing good service. Patron satisfaction can be linked to reference success.

A search of library literature shows little has been written on this. A great deal of useful information about training programs has been published. A large number of articles have been written dealing with the specifics of programs and services aimed at meeting the needs of the business patron. Several useful bibliographic tools have been published and serve both as collection development and finding aids. Still, from the literature, little attention has been given directly to training staff to be effective business librarians.

Most librarians in this field have learned by doing. For libraries to provide effective service, then, what are the necessary elements of a good training program?

The development of skilled staff requires attention to detail and a determined focus on the part of both staff and administration. Effective training depends upon the selection of suitable strategies, sound administrative control, and a well-sequenced series of steps that create good learning paths. As far back as the late 1960s, researchers were noting the importance of institutions to providing "organized learning experiences in a definite time period to increase the possibility of improving job performance growth."[2] This process, called human resource development, outlines learning experiences in terms of training, education, and development. Training and development are learning processes created by the job and the organization itself, while education is individually directed. Given the educational base of library school, what are some of the practicalities of learning business reference?

Successful programs create opportunities for the staff to learn and are based on a process of realization and familiarity. In sound training methods these elements are present. First, the organization creates an effective orientation process. Next, training in basic competencies and emphasis on acquiring subject depth takes place. A number of exercises and training aids are used. Last, a process of reaffirmation and measurement is undertaken.

Training staff to be effective reference librarians means first giving them a proper orientation to the task. Most institutions carry out formal or informal plans for what Woodard calls the "enculturation"[3] of new staff. These plans lay out the policies, walk staff through the physical environment, and describe internal procedures, etc. Staff is provided an opportunity to fit in socially with co-workers and adapt to their new surroundings. These plans are a good and necessary part of training. Staff can also benefit from some focused orientation to business patrons and characteristics of their questions.

Because of the newness of the subject matter and the general discomfort that working in a new area creates, it is important to provide some "cultural awareness" for staff in terms of the patrons they will deal with. One method I have used with some success is to meet one-on-one with new staff and describe some "typical" patrons and their searches. While business reference daily presents new challenges, repetition is readily apparent. Figure 1 shows the profile format I have used.

FIGURE 1. Orange County Library System Business and Science Department

Patron Profile: "Starting a business"

Question: "I need information on starting a business. Can you help me?"

Profile: Asker may be from any background but typically younger and unfamiliar with Libraries. Opening question is indicative of complex need. Information being sought may take many forms and range from search for ideas to questions about incorporation and funding. Initial exchange likely to lead to several follow up ones. Asker may be pressed for time and appear overwhelmed at complexity of sources. Referrals to outside agencies helpful part of process.

Sources: *Small Business Sourcebook; Starting and Operating Your Florida Business.* (No single source is perfect for each question. Particular need may dictate many other sources.)

In libraries everywhere patrons are asking for help in starting businesses, in researching companies, for stock market data, for job-hunting help and any number of other common questions. An often-unrecognized fact is that libraries have been providing assistance to business users for a long time. I have developed six or seven mini profiles of common patron types that I describe to new staff. The descriptions are aimed at teaching staff something of the "new culture" they will work in as well as making the task seem less intimidating. A profile covers the type question they ask, why they might ask it, what one or two major sources might help, and gives some characteristics of the user. In addition to the aforementioned, I have profiles of list makers, demographic researchers, marketing projects, and others.

In the manner a traveler to a foreign country gains by learning about the people, so too do reference librarians working with business subjects benefit from learning about the culture. One of the best learning tools available to librarians is the study of the questions our patrons ask us. This process, called question analysis, is defined by Miranda Pao as "the study of human information seeking behavior."[4] Pao cites a Rees and Saracevic model of the information seeking process.[5] The model suggests that patrons seek information in a movement from problem to need to question and ultimately to request. Characteristics of each state were described. Information seekers are confronted with problems and have no clear solution at hand. Each one of us constantly encounters information problems (defined as gaps in our knowledge) but there is generally no movement towards filling in the gap unless there is a motivational event, i.e., a desire to know.

One essential characteristic is that business patrons come to the library with strong motivating events; life forces are often at work. They want to start a new business, get a new job, make more money, etc. Often external pressures are brought to bear on the information need as well. They may be told by the "boss" to get the material; they may be under deadline pressure; it is a team project and their standing is at stake; or their own knowledge of the field is limited and they are counting on the library to make up the difference.

These factors, while not unique to business reference, help explain some of the behavior staff will encounter in working with these patrons. Patrons are more likely to be demanding, time sensitive, and carry high expectations about the results of the library visit regardless of their individual fluency with libraries.

In the Rees and Saracevic model the words "question" and "request" appear as essential concepts. As defined, a question is the patron's statement of the information need while a request is the restatement of that need based upon the interchange between librarian and patron.[5] This is a classic definition of a reference interview. It is the interchange that allows a librarian to identify suitable subject terms, and shape the raw question into a form that can be matched with an information source. Reference interviews are the key level for staff to be effective in helping generate patron satisfaction. Therefore it follows it is at this level that the bulk of training should take place.

Neglecting opportunities for staff to practice interviews on business subjects impedes their development. All too often the assumption is made that staff know how to interview properly. Understandably subject expertise improves interviews; therefore, exercises designed to complement both processes are important teaching tools. One sequence of training steps I have followed to help staff is to use guided sets of reference questions to help them learn the sources and their common uses, then role playing with peers acting as "typical" patrons to help them learn how to interview.

These training questions are developed around a theme. Typically a set might contain five or six questions on the same subject and are designed to force use of standard sources in different ways or to compare common sources. Figure 2 is an example of one such training set. Reference staff is given the opportunity to work through them at their own pace and to develop a better understanding of both the source and the type question.

Given a new terminology aspect of business reference, several of the practice sets deal with slang terms for reference tools or with terms often used in conjunction with a subject. Other exercises are intended to guide the staff through an exploration of the sources. For example, an exercise might ask only one question but call for five sources.

After staff has completed a practice set they discuss the results with an assigned peer. Their guides are encouraged to walk them through any area of uncertainty and to give their personal opinions as to the merit and use of a particular reference tool. This process helps cement relationships with co-workers and yields good insight into the tools.

Once staff begins to gain familiarity with the reference tools, they are ready to hone their interview skills. The critical point for both patron and staff is the reshaping of a question into a request. The most

FIGURE 2. Orange County Library System Business and Science Department

Practice Questions: Buzzwords

Here is a list of items we often get asked for by a slang name. See if you can match up an actual item with a slang name. In some cases an exact source is not possible. In those give the concept or subject matter.

Thomas

Means

SRDS

Pratt's

The Redbook or The Agency Redbook

Contacts Influential

Wards

D&B

S&P

Sweets

Ayers

Bacons

RMA

Bluebook

REDI

effective training allows staff to practice in a non-threatening environment. A number of techniques can be applied. Role playing with peers accomplishes many of the basic objectives.

When seasoned reference staff take on the role of a patron and draw from their experience, the trainee is able to work through common questions. One good exercise is to have each staff member play the role of a patron asking a typical question and then, after each question, allow for a period of discussion. We practice this without consulting the reference sources to reinforce recall of possible reference tools. In the best outcomes both interview skills and reference tool knowledge are enhanced. Other training practices include "shadowing" experienced staff with real patrons and having new staff open the interview with an experienced staff member observing and ready to offer assistance.

Given the critical nature of the training process for both patron and staff, it is important that effective controls be in place. Specific measurable objectives that "describe the kind of performance that will be accepted as evidence that the learner has mastered a particular task" are vital.[6] From an administrative point of view, the training allows the staff member to perform the job as described. From the practical view of the reference staff, the training allows them to perform the job as described–with lessened anxiety and heightened professional confidence.

It follows then that some mutual form of measure is best to assure the right outcomes for both parties. A number of tools can serve this purpose. Staff might be observed and critiqued after the training. Tests can be given to measure reference ability. Checklists can be employed to document the training process.

Given the complexity of the subject matter, checklists are an excellent choice. A well-designed checklist of training topics will assure staff get consistent exposure to each subject or tool. They can also be designed in a way for the trainee to indicate their own comfort level. A measure that indicates staff feels ready to "teach" another is a strong score. Figure 3 is taken from a checklist developed by staff to capture topics.

Short tests can be given to measure skill level and reinforce basics. In training I have given a set of twenty-five questions ranging from basic to mildly difficult. Scores of eighty-five percent indicate competent ground level understanding.

Administrative control over training is an important element in staff performance. As Woodard notes "training for reference staff should be a continuous process that is never really finished."[7] Both administrators and staff need to nurture the process. Continuous learning requires a number of activities as well as general staff desire. Workshops, professional readings, and conferences are external aids. Simple internal exercises can be beneficial too. Swapping "hard" questions at staff meetings and sharing favorite Websites are illustrations of on-the-job training.

The results of a good training program for business reference can not be overemphasized. The strong demand by patrons, the ever-changing nature of the field, and the abilities of staff are in constant interplay. Good outcomes will come about when staff are well-trained and well-equipped. With a good training program in place staff are better equipped to deal with this element of their job. And in a short time, what seemed like a journey to a distant and strange land, will become a ride down a very familiar road.

FIGURE 3. Business and Science Training Checklist

STAFF: _____

B&S DEPT.	INTRODUCED	FEEL COMFORTABLE	FLUENT
Photo-Copiers			
Micro-Fiche Readers			
Help-Wanted USA			
REDI			
Industry Standards			
Mil. Specs			
ASI			
Phone Fiche			
Misc. Fiche			
Map Case:			
FEMA Maps			
U.S. Geological Maps			
Nautical Maps			
Plat Maps			
Census Tracts			
Financial Table (List)			
Index Table			
Consumer Table			
Typing Room			
B&S Bulletin Board			

NOTES

1. Woodard, Beth S. "Reference Staff Training and Development," in *Reference and Information Services*, ed. Richard E. Bopp and Linda C. Smith (Englewood, CO: Libraries Unlimited, 1995), 185.

2. Nadler, Leonard and Zeace Nadler, *Handbook of Human Resource Development*, 2nd ed. (New York: John Wiley, 1990), 3.

3. Woodard, "Reference Staff Training and Development," 186.

4. Pao, Miranda L. *Concepts of Information Retrieval* (Englewood, CO: Libraries Unlimited, 1989), 168.

5. Pao, 169.

6. Pao, 173.

7. Woodard, "Reference Staff Training and Development," 192.

A Model Workshop to Increase Knowledge of African-American Reference Sources for Public Services Library Staff

Rudolph Clay, Jr.

SUMMARY. This article describes the planning, organization, and implementation of a reference workshop for public services staff of the St. Louis Public Library (St. Louis, MO), designed to increase their knowledge of African-American reference sources. Participant evaluations are analyzed and presented with recommendations for model modification and follow-up. *[Article copies available for a fee from The Haworth Document Delivery Service: 1-800-342-9678. E-mail address: getinfo@haworthpressinc. com <Website: http://www.haworthpressinc.com>]*

KEYWORDS. African-American, African-American studies, reference services, workshop

This article describes a two-hour workshop designed to increase public services staffs' knowledge of African-American reference sources and provide practice in constructing research strategies, and offers a bibliography to be utilized as a reference collection development tool. The workshop was presented to approximately 100 public

Rudolph Clay, Jr. is Head of the Olin Library Reference Department at Washington University. He holds an MALS from the University of Michigan.

Address correspondence to: Rudolph Clay, Jr., Olin Library, Reference Department, 1 Brookings Drive, Campus Box 1016, St. Louis, MO 63130.

[Haworth co-indexing entry note]: "A Model Workshop to Increase Knowledge of African-American Reference Sources for Public Services Library Staff." Clay, Rudolph, Jr. Co-published simultaneously in *Journal of Library Administration* (The Haworth Information Press, an imprint of The Haworth Press, Inc.) Vol. 29, No. 1, 1999, pp. 47-57; and: *Library Training for Staff and Customers* (ed: Sara Ramser Beck) The Haworth Information Press, an imprint of The Haworth Press, Inc., 2000, pp. 47-57. Single or multiple copies of this article are available for a fee from The Haworth Document Delivery Service [1-800-342-9678, 9:00 a.m. - 5:00 p.m. (EST). E-mail address: getinfo@haworthpressinc.com].

services staff of the St. Louis Public Library system. Four sessions were conducted over a two-week period with approximately twenty-five staff members attending each session. With modification, this workshop model can be replicated in other libraries to increase public services staffs' knowledge of African-American reference sources.

In its ongoing program to expand library staff knowledge and skills, the St. Louis Public Library maintains an active staff development program utilizing a variety of workshops and other training opportunities. This article will examine one effort to increase public services staff expertise in a specific subject area, African-American reference sources. The African-American Reference Committee of the St. Louis Public Library utilized a written survey to assess reference services to patrons inquiring about African-American topics. The committee surveyed public services staff of the main library and the fourteen branch libraries to determine patron characteristics, patron needs, and collection strengths and weaknesses in this subject area. The thirty-three completed surveys revealed that 20.2% of the African-American reference questions came from adults, 39.5% from teenagers and/or young adults, and 40.3% from children. Though most of the respondents felt that the collections met their clientele's needs, several collection gaps were identified:

- Age-related reference sources, especially for the primary grades;
- African-American inventors and their inventions;
- Biographical material on African-American athletes, mathematicians, musicians, scientists, and those in business;
- Current statistical information on African-Americans;
- Local African-American history.

When asked their opinion on how their branch/department could provide better African-American reference service, public services staff made the following responses:

- Acquire an African-American online database;
- Create separate African-American sections in the fiction and non-fiction collections;
- Catalog reference titles so that African-American titles are shelved close together on the reference shelves;
- Acquire additional circulating copies of books in the reference collection because patrons wanted to use them at home;

- Update the African-American reference titles already in the collection;
- Acquire additional African-American reference titles;
- Provide additional training in African-American references sources for public services staff.

Because additional training in African-American reference sources was identified as a factor that might improve reference services, the author was invited to meet with the American-American Reference Committee to discuss the possibility of designing a workshop to address these training issues. The author was selected because of his experience in teaching an undergraduate university research methods course in African and African-American Studies. A workshop was then developed with the following goals:

1. Assist public services staff in increasing their knowledge of African-American reference sources;
2. Provide practice in constructing research strategies for locating information in this subject area;
3. Present participants with an annotated bibliography of African-American reference sources that could be utilized as a reference collection development tool.

Approximately one hundred public services staff members attended a two-hour workshop entitled, "Reference Sources in African-American Studies." The workshops were held in four locations of the St. Louis Public Library system, over a two-week period. The workshop was divided into four major parts (Figure 1). The sessions began with an introduction of the facilitator followed by introductions of each participant. Participants' introductions were important because these public services staff worked in various departments and branches of the St. Louis Public Library system and had not all met. One objective of the workshop was to facilitate a collegial approach to answering reference questions, whereby other staff members were considered potential resources. It was also acknowledged that each participant brought to the workshop some experience in answering reference questions and that the sharing of this collective knowledge would be an integral component of the workshop's effectiveness.

The goals and structure of the workshop were then covered. As an icebreaker, participants were asked to take two minutes to think about

FIGURE 1. Workshop Structure

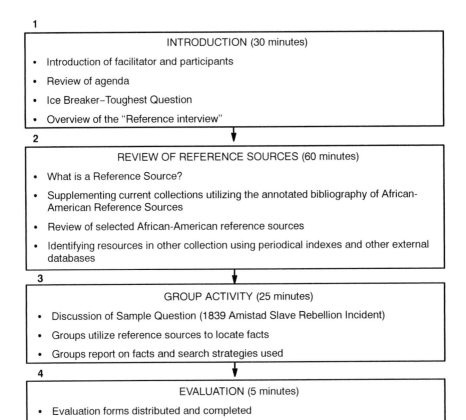

the toughest African-American related question they had received. Each participant then had an opportunity to state their question and the resource(s) they used to answer it. Most participants shared a question they had received and the sources they had consulted. This stimulated the beginnings of some informal exchanges between participants. The icebreaker successfully focused participants' attention on the workshop topic and allowed participants to quickly become actively involved in the workshop.

A brief overview of the reference interview was presented, as outlined in Jennerich's *The Reference Interview as Creative Art.*[1] The goal of the overview was to identify what Jennerich refers to as "the actor's tools" (verbal skills, nonverbal skills, interviewing techniques, and follow-up). It was stressed that the use of these tools assists in ensuring that the patron's inquiry has been correctly understood. The discussion lasted about fifteen minutes.

The second segment of the workshop focused on a review of approximately twenty African-American reference sources, divided into six major categories: encyclopedias, biographical sources, dictionaries and guides, statistical sources, atlases and maps, and newspaper and periodical indexes. Participants received an annotated bibliography of approximately seventy African-American reference sources (Appendix A contains the bibliography without annotations). This segment lasted one hour. Approximately ten minutes were spent on each category, emphasizing the general types of questions that could be answered by the representative titles. Participants were encouraged to share their previous knowledge of and experiences with the titles being discussed. This segment of the workshop ended with a discussion of using periodical indexes and external databases to identify potential resources outside of the local collections, when further information is needed.

The third segment of the workshop consisted of a twenty-minute small group exercise utilizing some of the sources that had been discussed. The groups consisted of six to seven participants. Each group was supplied with about six to eight reference sources and asked to compile as many facts as possible on the 1839 Amistad Slave Rebellion Incident. An entry on the Amistad Rebellion from *1001 Things Everyone Should Know About African American History* was distributed to provide some basic facts about the topic.[2] The purpose of the activity was to:

- Develop first hand experience with resources that may have been new to participants;
- Facilitate a collegial approach to locating information on African-American topics;
- Identify various strategies used to locate information.

The strategy used to locate information in the various resources was emphasized because each source was arranged somewhat differently. Some did not include an index and forced participants to use topical headings to locate the information. A few of the sources listed the information under "Joseph Cinque" rather than the name of the ship, Amistad. Variant spellings were used in different sources. Utilizing only one search strategy can often result in overlooking information that actually is contained in the source. After ten minutes of searching, the four groups were then asked to report on the facts they had discovered from each source used, and the strategy they had developed in looking for the information. Each successive group would report only new information or a search strategy that had not been previously mentioned. Discrepancies between sources in dates, spellings, and other facts were also noted. Participants were often surprised to discover from a colleague that a particular resource was already available in one part of the library system, but not in their collection.

EVALUATION RESULTS

According to the original plan, the last five minutes of the workshop were to be devoted to completing a one-page evaluation form. Because the workshops ran over their scheduled two-hour time period, participants were asked to complete the evaluation form and return it to the facilitator by mail (Appendix B). Only twenty evaluations (20%) were returned. Nineteen of the twenty returned evaluations stated that the participants "knew some of the material." Only one stated that "most of the material presented was new to me." When asked if the topic was adequately covered, eighteen indicated "yes," and two indicated "somewhat." All twenty evaluations indicated that the session had adhered to what was advertised. Eighteen participants rated the workshop handouts as "useful." Two participants rated the handouts as "somewhat useful." The workshop handouts included the following: the bibliography of African-American Reference Sources (Appendix A), a select bibliography of journals that review reference works, and a list of Amistad Internet sites. Thirteen participants rated the facilitator's presentation as "excellent," six rated it as "very good," and one rated it as "adequate."

RECOMMENDATIONS

The two-hour time frame should be extended to three hours to more adequately cover the content of the four sections. The first section, the

Introduction, should be extended from thirty minutes to forty minutes. This would allow ten minutes to be devoted to the overview of the reference interview. The Review of Reference Sources, the second section, should be extended from one hour to one and one-half hours. There was not adequate time to allow participants to discuss their previous use of the sources for specific questions. This can be an important component of the workshop because staff in various departments and branches of a library system often receive the same or similar questions.

A ten-minute break after the review of the sources would give participants a chance to relax and mingle with the other participants before the group exercise. Extending the third section, the group exercise, to thirty minutes would allow five additional minutes for group reports.

The evaluation form should be amended to include an overall rating of the workshop and a question assessing whether or not participants felt the workshop was beneficial. Many participants stated that a large number of questions are received from elementary and secondary school students before and during February, Black History Month. Since the workshop was conducted in December, a follow-up study in March may have provided evidence of the effectiveness of the workshop. The follow-up could have also assessed the effectiveness of the bibliography as a collection development tool.

CONCLUSION

Though the evaluations indicate that this workshop has the potential to be an effective staff development tool, some time adjustments are needed. It is hoped that this model can be adapted and replicated in other libraries to increase public services staff's knowledge of African-American reference sources.

NOTES

1. Elaine Z. Jennerich and Edward J. Jennerich, *The Reference Interview as a Creative Art* (Englewood, Colorado: Libraries Unlimited, 1997): 9-26.

2. Jeffrey C. Stewart, *1001 Things Everyone Should Know About African American History* (New York: Doubleday, 1996): 26-27.

APPENDIX A

African-American Reference Sources

ENCYCLOPEDIAS

African-American Encyclopedia. New York: Marshall Cavendish, 1993. 6 volumes.

Afro-American Encyclopedia. North Miami, Florida: Educational Book Publishers, 1974. 10 volumes.

Cambridge History of Africa. Cambridge: University Press, 1975-86. Volumes 1-8

Encyclopedia of African-American Culture and History. New York: Simon and Schuster, 1996.

Encyclopedia of Black America. New York: McGraw-Hill, 1981. 921 p.

Encyclopedia of Multiculturalism. New York: Marshall Cavendish, 1993. 6 volumes

General History of Africa. Berkeley: University of California Press, 1981- .

The Negro Almanac: A Reference Work on the Afro-American. New York: Wiley, 1983. 1550 p.

DICTIONARIES, GUIDES, AND HANDBOOKS

Africa South of the Sahara. London: Europa Publications. (an annual)

African American Almanac: A Day-by-Day Black History. Leon T. Ross and Kenneth A. Williams. Jefferson, N.C.: McFarland, 1997.

African American Historic Places: National Register of Historic Places. Washington, D.C.: National Park Service, United States Department of the Interior, 1994.

The African American Resource Guide to the Internet and Online Services. Stafford L. Battle and Rey O. Harris. New York: McGraw-Hill, 1996.

The African-American Yellow Pages: A Comprehensive Resource Guide and Directory. Edited by Stanton F. Biddle. New York: An Owl Book, 1996.

Black Americans: A Statistical Sourcebook. Palo Alto, CA: Information Publications.

Black Chronology from 4,000 B.C. to the Abolition of the Slave Trade. Boston, G.K. Hall, 1983. 312 p.

In Black and White: A Guide to Magazine Articles, Newspaper Articles, and Books Concerning More Than 15,000 Black Individuals and Groups. Detroit, Michigan: Gale Research Company, 1980. 3 volumes.

Black Elected Officials: A National Roster. New York: Joint Center for Political Studies.

The Black Resource Guide. Washington: Ben Johnson, 1988-1989. 285 p.

The Chronological History of the Negro in America. New York: Harper, 1969. 698 p.

Contemporary Quotations in Black. Compiled and Edited by Anita King. Westport, Connecticut: Greenwood Press, 1997.

The Dictionary of Afro-Latin American Civilization. Westport, Connecticut: Greenwood Press, 1980.

Hippocrene U.S.A. Guide to the Historic Black South: Historical Sites, Cultural Centers, and Musical Happenings of the African-American South. New York: Hippocrene Books, 1993.

Historical Dictionary of the Civil Rights Movement. Ralph E. Luker (Historical Dictionaries of Religions, Philosophies, and Movement, No. 11) Lanham, Md: Scarecrow Press, 1997.

The Middle East and North Africa. London: Europa Publications. (an annual)

One Thousand And One Things Everyone Should Know About African American History. New York: Doubleday, 1996.

The Social and Economic Status of the Black Population In the United States: A Historical View, 1790-1978. (Current Population Reports: Special Studies: Series P-23; No. 80) Washington, D.C.: U.S. Government Printing Office, 1979.

The State of Black America. New York: National Urban League, 1988.

The Timetables of African-American History: A Chronology of the Most Important People and Events in African-American History. New York: Simon and Schuster, 1995.

Timelines of African-American History: 500 Years of Black Achievement. New York: Perigee Books, 1994.

BIOGRAPHICAL SOURCES

The Black 100: A Ranking of the Most Influential African-Americans, Past and Present. Columbus Salley. New York: Citadel, 1994.

Black Saga: The African American Experience. Charles M. Christian. New York: Houghton Mifflin,1995.

Contemporary Black Biography: Profiles of the International Black Community. Detroit: Gale, 1992- .

Dictionary of American Negro Biography. Edited by Rayford W. Logan and Michael R. Winston. New York: Norton, 1982.

Facts on File Encyclopedia of Black Women In America. Edited by Darlene Clark Hine. New York: Facts on File, 1997.

Freedom's Lawmakers: A Directory of Black Officeholders During Reconstruction. Eric Foner. Baton Rouge, LA: Louisiana State University Press, 1996.

In Black and White: A Guide to Magazine Articles, Newspaper Articles, and Books Concerning More Than 15,000 Black Individuals and Groups. Detroit, Michigan: Gale Research Company, 1980, 3 volumes.

Who's Who Among Black Americans. Northbrook, Illinois: Who's Who Among Black Americans, Inc., 1988.

Index to Black Periodicals. New York: G.K. Hall, 1984- . (annual)

Bibliographic Guide to Black Studies. New York: Schomburg Center for Research in Black Culture and G.K. Hall (Boston). 1975- . (annual)

Black Index: Afro-Americana in Selected Periodicals, 1907-1949. Richard Newman. New York: Garland, 1981.

Black Newspaper Index. Ann Arbor, Michigan: University Microfilms International. 1971- . (quarterly)

Index to St. Louis Newspapers. St. Louis, MO: St. Louis Public Library. 1975-1979. (annual)

Kaiser Index to Black Resources. 1948-1986/from the Schomburg Center for Research in Black Culture of the New York Public Library. Brooklyn, N.Y. : Carlson, 1992. 5 v.

SUMMARIES OF CURRENT EVENTS

African Recorder: A Fortnightly Record of African Events with Index. New Delhi, 1962-. (published every two weeks)

Africa Research Bulletin. Exeter, England: Africa Research Ltd, 1964-. (published monthly)

ATLASES AND MAPS

Africa Today: An Atlas of Reproducible Pages. Wellesley, MA: Editors of World Eagle, Inc., 1983,153 p.

African History in Maps. Essex, England: Longman, 1982. 76 p.

The Atlas of Africa. New York: Free Press, 1973, 335 p.

The Historical and Cultural Atlas of African Americans. Molefi K. Asante and Mark T. Mattson. New York: Macmillan, 1991.

Historical Maps on File. New York: Facts on File, 1984.

Nigeria in Maps. New York: Africana Publishing Company, 1982,148 p.

APPENDIX B

Reference Sources in African-American Studies
Workshop Evaluation from Summary

1. Did the content of the session adhere to what was advertised?

   Yes   <u>20</u>   Somewhat ____   No _____

2. Was the topic adequately covered?

   Yes   <u>18</u>   Somewhat   <u>2</u>   No _____

3. Please rate the instructor's presentation.

   Excellent <u>13</u>   Very Good   <u>6</u>   Adequate <u>1</u>   Inadequate _____

4. Do you think the handouts are/will be useful to you?

   Yes   <u>18</u>   Somewhat   <u>2</u>   No _____

5. How much of the information presented were things you were familiar with already?

   I already knew most of this   _____

   I know some of the material   <u>19</u>

   Most of the material presented was new to me   <u>1</u>

Fully Disclosed Yet Merely Descriptive: Intricacies of Training the Patent and Trademark Information Professional

Martha Crockett Sneed

SUMMARY. Training is a key focus for the U.S. Patent and Trademark Office (USPTO) administration of its nationwide network of eighty-three Patent and Trademark Depository Libraries (PTDLs). With ever-widening access to patent and trademark data through a variety of print and electronic media, training is what differentiates the public service expectations at a PTDL from all other libraries. The author will explore two primary training vehicles employed by the USPTO in building intellectual property knowledge management skills in PTDL librarians. These librarians are evolving into highly specialized patent and trademark information experts, a newly developing area of library expertise. *[Article copies available for a fee from The Haworth Document Delivery Service: 1-800-342-9678. E-mail address: getinfo@haworthpressinc.com <Website: http:// www.haworthpressinc.com>]*

Martha Crockett Sneed has worked with patent and trademark information service delivery to public users for more than twenty-three years. She is Manager of the Patent and Trademark Depository Library (PTDL) Program at the U.S. Patent and Trademark Office (USPTO), where she has worked since 1985. She served at the Detroit Public Library from 1973-1984 as a sci-tech and government documents reference librarian and assistant department head. While there, she also served as the PTDL liaison to the USPTO for seven years. Martha received her AB from the University of Michigan and her MSLS from Wayne State University.

Address correspondence to: Martha Crockett Sneed, Manager, Patent and Trademark Depository Library Program, U.S. Patent and Trademark Office, Crystal Park 3-Suite 461, Washington, DC 20231 (E-mail: martha.sneed@uspto.gov).

[Haworth co-indexing entry note]: "Fully Disclosed Yet Merely Descriptive: Intricacies of Training the Patent and Trademark Information Professional." Sneed, Martha Crockett. Co-published simultaneously in *Journal of Library Administration* (The Haworth Information Press, an imprint of The Haworth Press, Inc.) Vol. 29, No. 1, 1999, pp. 59-78; and: *Library Training for Staff and Customers* (ed: Sara Ramser Beck) The Haworth Information Press, an imprint of The Haworth Press, Inc., 2000, pp. 59-78. Single or multiple copies of this article are available for a fee from The Haworth Document Delivery Service [1-800-342-9678, 9:00 a.m. - 5:00 p.m. (EST). E-mail address: getinfo@haworthpressinc.com].

KEYWORDS. Training, information, patents, trademarks, Patent and Trademark Depository Libraries, PTDLs, fellowship, intellectual property, U.S. Patent and Trademark Office, PTO, USPTO, librarian

INTRODUCTION

The Patent and Trademark Depository Library Program (PTDLP) under the U.S. Patent and Trademark Office (USPTO) administers a nationwide network of eighty-three academic, public, and state libraries designated as Patent and Trademark Depository Libraries (PTDLs) under *Title 35, United States Code, Section 13.* Published service standards for the program require that PTDLs provide assistance to the public in the efficient use of patent and trademark collections and their associated information access tools. It is not enough for a PTDL to simply maintain source documents or provide access to electronic data. PTDLs must build staff knowledge management skills in the intellectual property arena in order to assist public users in meeting their information needs and improving their basis for making sound business decisions. To help PTDLs meet this standard, the PTDL Program at the USPTO provides a number of training opportunities for PTDL librarians.

One such opportunity is an annual week-long training seminar held on-site at the USPTO, designed specifically for PTDL librarians. Another is a unique Fellowship Program in which PTDL staff librarians work in the program office at the USPTO's Arlington, Virginia headquarters for durations of up to two years. These training programs have been in place for twenty-one years and fifteen years respectively. Libraries and librarians working on a daily basis with the PTDL Program have witnessed tremendous growth in the importance of intellectual property to the U.S. and world economies. An offshoot of that growth is the development of a new specialty, patent and trademark librarianship. PTDLs which function as the only field presence of the PTO, are relied on for unique collections, services, and expertise of their library staffs. Carefully tailored USPTO support for multiple training strategies effects the development of this expertise.

DEFINITION OF A PATENT
AND TRADEMARK DEPOSITORY LIBRARY (PTDL)

A Patent and Trademark Depository Library, or PTDL, refers to a library which has entered into a formal relationship with the USPTO to assist the agency with the dissemination of patent and trademark information to public users. The statutory authority for what is now known as the Patent and Trademark Depository Library Program (PTDLP) rests in *Title 35, United States Code, Section 13* which allows for the distribution of patent copies to libraries for an annual statutory fee of fifty dollars. This 1871 statute has changed little over the past 128 years. What has changed is the dissemination strategy and information technology employed to effectively carry out the intent of the statute.

As mentioned in the Introduction, the network of libraries designated by the Commissioner of the Patent and Trademark Office as PTDLs currently consists of eighty-three public, academic and state libraries located in all fifty states, the District of Columbia and Puerto Rico. (See Appendix I.) In the first century of implementing the statute, the USPTO designated twenty-two libraries, mostly public, located primarily in the eastern and midwestern United States in areas of dense population and industry. Beginning in 1977, the USPTO directed expansion efforts to identify and designate at least one PTDL in every state, and began to increase utilization of academic and state libraries in addition to public libraries to carry out its strategy. This goal was achieved twenty years later in 1997. New strategic direction for expansion to the PTDLP calls for additional controlled growth in areas of high population combined with high patent and trademark activity which warrant the resources invested by the USPTO into each and every PTDL.

The USPTO, an agency under the Department of Commerce, is a headquarters-only agency with no field or regional offices. It regards the PTDL network as its field presence and fully utilizes PTDLs to increase awareness in and the use of intellectual property systems. In 1995, the USPTO began a new program to enter into business partnerships with selected PTDLs to introduce a heightened presence in their regions. Called Partnership PTDLs, they are located at the already established PTDLs in Detroit, Houston and Sunnyvale and are offering enhanced fee-based services over and above traditional PTDL services.[1] The Partnership Program is mentioned to illustrate the seriousness with which the USPTO regards its dissemination business and the critical role which PTDLs play in assisting the PTO with its mission.

PTDL SERVICE STANDARDS

A number of commitments are made by a library wishing to be designated as a PTDL. Standards outlining these commitments are set forth in a USPTO brochure entitled *Notes on Becoming a Patent and Trademark Depository Library,* which may be found on the PTO Website at: www.uspto.gov/go/ptdl. Following is a brief summary of standards which a library must meet as a PTDL, and why.

Acquire a Twenty-Year Backfile of U.S. Patents Going Back from the Year of PTDL Designation

The term of a U.S. patent is twenty years from date of filing. A twenty-year backfile of patents will therefore provide a collection of U.S. patents for public searching which are currently in force and not yet in the public domain.[2] Having access to an external online collection of U.S. patents is not sufficient to meet this requirement. PTDLs must be able to independently function as service providers for U.S. patents. Approximately forty percent of all PTDLs maintain complete collections of U.S. patents dating back to 1790. While a twenty-year backfile is a good beginning, the statutes for patentability require novelty. Therefore, searching a complete collection of U.S. patents yields a more accurate patentability search.

Provide Free Public Access to all Depository Materials

This standard is worded in such a way as to require that PTDLs provide a way for public users to view all depository materials for free, but still allow the PTDL the ability to charge for photocopying or generating computer printouts.

Protect the Integrity of Depository Collections So That They Remain Available to the Public

Materials provided by the USPTO to PTDLs must be organized, well-cared for, and maintained for public access. With rare exceptions, depository materials are non-circulating as they must be available for use whenever a user contacts the library for the information.

Maintain Collections of Classification Systems and Related Search Systems and Materials Which Are Critical to the Effective Utilization of Patent and Trademark Source Documents

This standard acknowledges that mere ownership of source documents is not sufficient to assist users of patent and trademark information. Effective access to source documents relies on the utilization of respective classification systems, electronic search systems and related materials designed to address the numerous ways in which a user approaches the information.

Retain Depository Materials Until, at the Initiative of the Library, Disposal of Them Has Been Arranged Through the USPTO. The USPTO Retains the Right of First Refusal to Acquire any Materials from the Library Which Were Provided Under the Provisions of the Statute

This is a statement of USPTO ownership of all materials provided on a depository basis, until such ownership is released by the USPTO.

Assist the Public in the Efficient Use of the Patent and Trademark Collections and Associated Information Access Tools

This standard sets forth the service differentiation associated with PTDL designation. A PTDL is required to actively engage the public user in a dialogue of what is needed, and then direct or guide the user to the appropriate resources. While a non-PTDL library may have patent and trademark materials obtained through other sources, a PTDL is mandated to provide high-level reference service by virtue of its depository association with the USPTO. "The buck stops here" is the intended motto for a PTDL with regard to its patent and trademark depository collections. PTDLs are libraries to which other libraries refer patrons for additional assistance.

Support Attendance for a Library Representative at Every Annual PTDL Training Seminar

The legal implications of providing reference services in the area of intellectual property require regular updating on new laws, treaties and procedures, and refreshing reference skills peculiar to the subject matter. It is therefore a requirement for a PTDL to send a representative to each annual training seminar.

Only by applying these service standards can the USPTO be assured of standardized, consistent and accurate reference service delivery at the PTDLs. They are the single commonality uniting all PTDLs.

THE INCREASED NEED FOR TRAINING

Since 1977, the year which marked the beginning of the second wave of libraries seeking designation as a PTDL, the number of libraries with PTDL status has grown from twenty-two to eighty-three. From a training perspective, the demands for keeping pace with this large increase in member institutions have been the subject of numerous discussions and meetings both at the USPTO and at the libraries. While the outcome of these discussions has resulted in the implementation of several meaningful training strategies, the pace of technology and the increased access to the information is relentlessly pushing forward the search for a greater variety of training solutions to meet the unique needs of the PTDL network. An underlying important refrain to keep in mind throughout this paper, is that PTDL service delivery is not easy. It is labor intensive at the reference desk, and the potential for negative outcomes for users provided with incorrect information can have a dramatic impact on their finances or their ability to seek available protection.

Some of the issues driving decisions on training mechanisms are worth pointing out. The PTDL Program encompasses eighty-three different libraries, each having distinct policies, missions, priorities, strategic directions and governing bodies and officials. Therefore, training needs to be planned against a backdrop of significant variety in library type and infrastructure. While each PTDL is expected to provide the name of a liaison to the USPTO (called a PTDL Representative) and that person is often the key provider of reference support for PTDL services in the institution, there are usually several librarians and some support staff at each PTDL who also provide service to patrons. Therefore, there is a variety in numbers of staff, job responsibilities, and job classifications of employees expected to have some knowledge about PTDL-related services within any given PTDL. Training for all of them needs to be part of a planned strategy to ensure accurate service delivery. Although the PTDL Program has been fortunate to have a good number of seasoned PTDL Representatives holding their positions for a number of years, there is the usual attrition due to promotion, retirement and relocation which creates a never ending pool of librarians requiring beginning training in the subject matter of patents and trademarks, not an easy subject matter to tame. Training needs encompass a demand for a variety of knowledge levels, from the raw novice to the expert, from the paraprofessional to the professional.

Another factor resulting in an increased need for training is that the strength of intellectual property systems nationally and internationally has grown dramatically over the past fifteen years, creating a heightened demand for information. A search through the literature on the importance and power of patents and trademarks will reveal potential reasons for the increase. Some attribute its growing importance to the 1982 establishment of the Court of Appeals for the Federal Circuit (CAFC) which has jurisdiction over all patent appeals from various district courts as well as appeals from boards of the USPTO, resulting in more informed decisions. Some cite the efforts of national intellectual property offices and international organizations to harmonize worldwide intellectual property rights, resulting in new laws and treaties which strengthen those rights. Also, in 1982, the USPTO Commissioner was elevated to the status of Assistant Secretary of Commerce. These factors, combined with the successful automation efforts of the USPTO and the streamlining and reengineering of internal processes and procedures, have resulted in the perception that obtaining appropriate protections for intellectual property is very often a sound business decision. As an agency which receives all of its funding from user fees, customer responsiveness is imperative for the USPTO. The result is that more patents are being granted and more federal trademarks are being registered than ever before. In fiscal year 1982, there were 124,800 patent applications and 73,621 trademark applications filed at the USPTO. In fiscal year 1997, there were 237,045 patent applications and 224,355 trademark applications filed at the USPTO.[3]

Whatever the reasons may be, the use of intellectual property protections is steadily on the increase each year, with very dramatic jumps in years when new laws come into effect which change filing requirements. It has become ever more vital to obtain pertinent and accurate intellectual property information in a timely fashion, so it is no news that the proliferation of electronic patent and trademark resources over the past several years has stimulated a quantum leap in awareness of intellectual property systems overall. This can be a fairly dangerous situation from a public user standpoint when making decisions about patentability, infringement or filing applications. Because of the Internet, many more people know a very little bit about a complex subject than ever before. They may know just enough to get themselves into trouble. While many libraries have ready availability to the data, the PTDLs are the libraries to which patrons should be directed for other than basic assistance because they are backed by the power of a federal agency mandated to provide protections for intellectual property. PTDLs are empowered by the USPTO to manage knowledge of intellectual property information, a far cry from mere access to data.

The key to our training solution at the USPTO therefore becomes one that mimics the philosophy of the USPTO's information dissemination strategy, which is to provide information in a variety of formats to suit the needs of a variety of customers. The USPTO also attempts to provide a variety of training products and services to meet the needs of an ever-expanding pool of librarians, institutions, and users who require the training. Current training mechanisms supplied by the USPTO to PTDLs include the following: sponsoring public information seminars on-site at PTDLs to train potential PTDL users (an excellent way to train PTDL librarians in public user expectations); conducting staff training on-site at a new PTDL as a component of preparing the new PTDL for operational status; providing one-on-one training at the USPTO at the request of a PTDL; producing training videotapes;[4] producing information handouts and brochures which can be used as is or tailored by a library; maintaining an updated Website and providing guidance to PTDLs on their PTDL-specific Web page content; handling daily reference requests from PTDLs in an instructional mode; offering video conference lectures conducted by USPTO experts; distributing all USPTO newsletters to PTDLs which often contain historical information, search hints on automated systems, and recommendations of particular data bases for particular search queries; and encouraging and supporting the development of additional training mechanisms by PTDLs themselves. Because training is so central to the core business of PTDLP, our attention is constantly trained on mechanisms for improvement. The development of multimedia training tools is our next focus.

Two of our most enduring and successful training components will now be explored in some detail, first the annual PTDL training seminar, followed by the PTDL Fellowship Program.

ANNUAL TRAINING SEMINAR FOR PTDL LIBRARIANS

On December 18, 1974, William I. Merkin, then Assistant Commissioner for Administration, United States Patent and Trademark Office, sent a letter to the twenty-two United States Patent Depository Libraries (PDLs)[5] requesting information on "what public use is made of the files of U.S. patents distributed to U.S. libraries under the provisions of 35 USC 13." Following that initial inquiry, the first of what was to become annual conferences for the nation's PDL representatives was held at the PTO on April 18, 19 and 20, 1977.[6]

Who can say when a workplace event, when repeated on a regular basis, evolves from an expectation, to a tradition, and finally to a service standard? From the author's personal experience in being involved with most of the annual PTDL training seminars since 1977, and comparing it to other ways in which training is conducted in libraries and in the federal government, this evolutionary process is most successful when everyone understands the mission, works directly with the mission and has passion for carrying out the mission. The PTDL Program is fortunate to have a very clear mission, a very defined group of people tasked to carry it out both at the USPTO and in each of the eighty-three PTDLs, and a sincere desire to make it work.

The groundwork established during the first 1977 conference formed a solid structure for the following years of PTDL Program growth, and the foundation for excellent communications between the PTDLs and the USPTO. During that first conference, librarians from seventeen of the twenty-two PDLs had a chance for direct interaction with USPTO experts and officials. The librarians received training in searching patents using paper-based systems and were questioned about their needs to improve access to the patent information at their libraries. They found out about search tools they did not know existed, they provided input on how to improve USPTO publications, they were able to talk to decision makers at the USPTO, and they were able to network with each other regarding their very well-defined responsibilities. At the end of three days, they knew they wanted to come back again, and the USPTO recognized how important it was that they keep coming back. Now, twenty-two years later, the annual training seminars are critical to the successful administration of the PTDL Program.

The author is grateful for an opportunity to explain the importance of the annual training seminars for the benefit of library directors, department heads, administrators, officials, and reference librarians who have not had the opportunity to experience one first hand. Our annual training seminars keep the attenders together all day long for a full week. While there are some concurrent training opportunities afforded to address varying levels of expertise, the expectation from the USPTO is that the attendee needs to be there at all sessions. Oddly enough, there has never been a need to state this to attending librarians. It must be a self-evident deduction based on observing the relatively small size of the group, the familiarity of USPTO staff with all names and faces from the PTDLs, the overall camaraderie of the group and the uniqueness of the subject matter at hand. Who would want to be anywhere else?! If we have a fault, it is that we do not provide any opportunities for getting a taste of Washington, DC. Ask anyone who has attended a PTDL annual training seminar about the intensity of the experience. It cannot be equated with an annual national association conference where the focus is on personal professional development and attendance at sessions is a matter of individual choice. The PTDL annual training seminar is key to surviving the year in between seminars.

Today, the annual training seminars have settled into a March time frame, and have become a full five days with a sixth day of optional training for libraries with access to special data bases. There are an average of forty-five different presentations dispersed over these six days. While the topics and specific structure change a little every year, there are things common to all the seminars. First, because the seminars are held on the USPTO campus, all sessions are taught by practicing USPTO experts. Standard seminar instructors include Patent Examining Group Directors, Trademark Staff Attorneys from the Assistant Commissioner of Trademarks office, specialized patent examiners in plants and designs or in specialized arts such as computer-related inventions or biotechnology, patent classification experts who instruct in the intricacies of the U.S. Patent Classification System and related search systems, and the information specialists who design the electronic search tools specifically for the PTDLs.

Because of the USPTO's frequent rules changes or new laws impacting procedures or practice, special instructors are needed every year depending on what has changed. In the past, these have included attorneys from USPTO policy areas, petition attorneys, specialists from the area of the USPTO which administers and maintains the patent bar roster, legislative and international affairs staff, librarians from USPTO's internal libraries, officials from the Office of Budget and Long-Range Planning, and experts on the USPTO's educational outreach efforts. Finally, time is built in every year for access to USPTO appointed or senior officials who take a keen interest in the USPTO's only field representatives, the PTDL librarians. Nothing can replace this face time for impacting and affecting the level of support needed by PTDLs. Every year, in addition to the multitude of opportunities provided to PTDL librarians to make their needs or perspective directly known to the USPTO expert in question, there is also time built in for an open forum where librarians can ask any questions they choose related to their PTDL-related programs and services.

Other planned events may include vendors exhibits specific to intellectual property, hands-on training on automated systems, demonstrations of upcoming new systems, and opportunities for information exchange among the librarians themselves. The Patent and Trademark Depository Library Association, a recent American Library Association affiliate, hosts their annual meeting during the seminar week, and actively facilitates this information exchange in addition to sponsoring programs related to their service delivery which the USPTO is unable to host.

The USPTO gears up for the annual training seminar and uses the time frame between seminars to address issues raised at the previous seminar. So much new material is prepared for and distributed during this week in March, that the USPTO provides pre-labeled jiffy bags and mails everything back by overnight mail so that librarians can have the information at hand the first day they return to the workplace. Why is this so important? One of the training strategies mentioned earlier is to address the needs of other staff who offer service delivery and who cannot attend the annual seminar. Librarians who do attend are expected to instruct appropriate staff about all they have learned on their return. The sooner this is done, the better. For this reason, the USPTO attempts to get the seminar information out to the PTDLs fast.

If any one USPTO effort to support the PTDLs can be identified as having had the greatest impact on the history of PTDLP, it would be the annual training seminar. Because of needs expressed at seminars over the years by PTDL librarians, PTDLs have had a toll-free line to PTDLP for their use alone since 1983, a closed e-mail system since 1982 (prior to the currently-used Internet mailing list), improved search tools, computer equipment provided by the USPTO, and a database developed for their use, called Cassis.

Planning for each seminar begins as soon as the previous seminar concludes. The USPTO seminar planning team functions as an ongoing year-round team. Evaluations are carefully tabulated and reviewed to continue refining the seminar product. Attention to detail is paramount and feedback on individual concerns is provided. While the PTDL must provide the funding only for sending a representative to this required training event, there are no training dollars better spent for the value attained.

FELLOWSHIP PROGRAM FOR PTDL LIBRARIANS

An innovative program for bringing librarians from the "field" to the USPTO to work for specified periods of time was first implemented in 1983. It is often noted that necessity stimulates creative thinking. This is certainly true of the PTDL Fellowship Program. In 1982, the USPTO had only recently named a staff person whose sole function was to administer and develop the PTDL Program. That person was Carole A. Phillips (now Shores), who, by the time of her retirement in 1996, provided over twenty years of leadership to the PTDL Program. In 1982, she had one support employee to assist her in administering the burgeoning PTDL Program. As her background was not in librarianship, she sought to bring a professional librarian with work experience at a PTDL to her staff. Since hiring procedures in place at the time resulted in fairly lengthy recruitment processes, she identified and utilized the Intergovernmental Personnel Act (IPA) as a means to quickly bring a PTDL librarian to the USPTO. An additional benefit in using the IPA was and is that an individual working under the IPA does not count against the FTE (full-time equivalent) ceilings imposed on federal agencies. Fellowship librarians do not take up valuable FTE slots.

The IPA provides for the reassignment of employees of state or local governments or institutions of higher learning to facilitate federal-state-local cooperation through the short-term assignment of skilled manpower for periods of up to two years. It is the vehicle which has allowed the USPTO to bring sixteen PTDL librarians from the field to the USPTO over the past fifteen years. Since the PTDL network consists entirely of large public libraries, state libraries and institutions of higher learning, the IPA remains a fitting and ideal vehicle for the temporary reassignment of staff from this ready pool of qualified librarians. Through the IPA, the USPTO reimburses the home library for the salary and benefits of the librarian being reassigned, relocation expenses to and from the home library, and a housing stipend. The librarian continues to receive paychecks from the home library so that employment tenure remains intact. The librarian remains an employee of the home library, but works for the USPTO in a temporary reassignment status.

Backing up again to the year 1983, the USPTO sent a letter to the thirty-five PTDLs in the network at that time, advertising and seeking applicants for the first Fellowship. In the February 23, 1983, letter of invitation from William S. Lawson, the USPTO's Administrator for Documentation, the following paragraph identified the anticipated benefits in offering Fellowship: "The concept is to attract a PDL[5] professional who would be willing to come to Washington and assist in the work of our expanding PDL program. Such an individual could bring to the position the first-hand knowledge of the needs and operations of a PDL and, while at the PTO, learn about the functions of the Office in general, and the PDL Program in particular. Our hope is that the resulting 'cross fertilization' of experience would serve to guide the growth and enrichment of the PDL Program."

The basis for the PTDL Fellowship was then, and remains today, one of "cross fertilization." Librarians who have applied and been selected for the PTDL Fellowship have all lent their respective expertise toward the daily support of the PTDL Program and in developing new projects and initiatives to enhance the network as a whole. There is no doubt that the USPTO has been uniquely enriched by the presence of a highly qualified series of professionals who understand end-user support and customer service and translate this perspective for USPTO designers of systems, services and products who enjoy no direct contact with public users. The USPTO is definitely a winner in this regard.

But the home library is a winner, too. The Fellowship Program returns librarians to their home institutions forever changed by their experience at the USPTO. They receive many training opportunities, including training in all the automated and office computer systems which they must use on a daily basis, in addition to sitting in on the Patent and Trademark Academies which train new patent examiners and trademark examining attorneys. They return with a much higher level of knowledge about patents, trademarks and intellectual property overall, first-hand work experience in a large federal bureaucracy, an abundance of new agency and governmental contacts to assist them with their daily responsibilities or in undertaking new projects on their return to their home library, and most importantly, a larger view of the PTDL Program. The Fellowship librarians typically have travel opportunities, and over the course of a year may visit a number of PTDLs to conduct staff training or make presentations at public seminars. From these site visits, and from the daily exposure in the work environment, the overall importance of what the USPTO is attempting to accomplish through the nationwide PTDL Program begins to emerge.

Their contributions as a group have been numerous. Fellowship librarians were responsible for implementing the Cassis CD-ROM pilot in 1987 and 1988, implementing the trademark CD-ROM pilot in 1991, planning for the implementation of the Automated Patent System pilot to the PTDLs, and actually traveling to the fourteen sites to install and make the system operational, developing field definitions for CD-ROM trademark products, developing a subject index to all memoranda and e-mail, developing and maintaining the comprehensive *Directory of Patent and Trademark Depository Libraries,* and editing *AD LIBS, the Newsletter of the Patent and Trademark Depository Library Program.* For the past several years, the Fellows have specialized in either patents or trademarks. For these Fellows, an additional responsibility has been serving as the PTDLP liaison to the respective sites of the USPTO. Any one of the past PTDL Fellows will testify to the impact of the experience on their work afterwards. The USPTO continues to encourage interest in this unique program for PTDL librarians and hopes to continue building the expertise of the newly-developing specialty of patent and trademark librarianship.

Appendix II honors the librarians who were selected as PTDL Fellowship Librarians. Their home institutions, which deserve high praise for their support of this very special program, are also featured.

THE FUTURE OF INTELLECTUAL PROPERTY LIBRARIANSHIP AS A SPECIALTY

Having had the unique opportunity to be involved with the subject matter of patent and trademark information service delivery in a PTDL setting for over twenty years, this section will merely record the author's observations regarding the development and growth of a new librarian specialty, that of the patent and trademark librarian, or the intellectual property librarian.

The increase in the number of librarians who know more than a little about intellectual property has been fostered by the development and growth of the PTDL Program. The PTDL Program has, in turn, achieved a measure of success by both listening to and guiding the PTDL librarians. It is a productive cycle, with excellent service to the public as its overarching theme.

It has been a true benefit to have university libraries join the PTDL Program because of their encouragement to librarians to achieve tenure status, where possible, through active professional association involvement, submitting papers for publication, writing books and making presentations. Many of our PTDL Representatives, while not limited in their daily work to the delivery of PTDL services, have identified PTDL services as an untapped area for documenting the challenges of service delivery for the fulfillment of requirements related to tenure. This has helped to get citations into the literature and to raise the awareness of the specialty.

Not to be outdone, public and state librarians have devoted themselves to developing very fine user aids to make their lives easier at the highly charged reference desk. They have developed excellent staff training curricula for new librarians slated to work with PTDL services, and developed unique information-finding aids along with their colleagues in the university environment. As a group they have contributed much to the reputation of the PTDL Program with their hard, dedicated work over the past twenty years. They have shaped their new profession and fine-tuned it with networking facilitated by the USPTO.

Now, when a vacancy opens up in a PTDL, there are job announcements seeking "Patent Librarians." The USPTO has made an effort to collect the beginnings of a PTDL librarian job description file to assist PTDLs when vacancies do occur. When positions open up for engineering librarians or government publication librarians, one sees a requirement for experience with patents and trademarks with ever greater frequency. PTDLP often assists with PTDL vacancies by posting them on the dedicated PTDL mailing list. There has been some movement of PTDL librarians within the network which has been extremely advantageous for new libraries in the PTDL Program seeking experienced librarians, and for PTDL librarians wishing to relocate for various reasons.

New developments in the profession reflect what is happening in the larger world of intellectual property. Right now, that trend is growth. Watch for developments in the field by tracking the progress of the Patent and Trademark Depository Library Association. A Website is forthcoming!

NOTES

1. Partnership PTDLs include the Great Lakes Patent and Trademark Center (GLPTC) at the Detroit Public Library, the South Central Intellectual Property Partnership at Rice (SCIPPR), in Houston, and the Sunnyvale Center for Innovation, Invention and Ideas (SC[I]3, in California.

2. The only exceptions are patents whose terms have been extended under the Patent Term Restoration Act for patents going through the Food and Drug Administration (FDA) approval process, and those whose owners have not paid maintenance fees to maintain them for the full 20 years.

3. Patent and trademark applications filing statistics may be found in each year's annual report of the Commissioner for Patents and Trademarks.

4. The videotape entitled *Conducting a Patent Search at a PTDL* was designed to ease the burden of repetitive questions during an initial reference interview with a first-time public user. Ideally it should be utilized with every new patron. This is done effectively at the Akron-Summit County Public Library, for example. The videotape is available at all PTDLs for viewing, and is available for purchase from the PTO. See the PTO Website for more information.

5. PDL stands for Patent Depository Library. Trademarks were not incorporated into the mission of this dissemination program until 1991. In 1991, PDLs became known as PTDLs, Patent and Trademark Depository Libraries.

6. This paragraph, written by David Morrison, 13th PTDL Fellowship Librarian, was taken from *AD LIBS, the Newsletter of the Patent and Trademark Depository*

Library Program, 18 (no.1): 1 (March 1997). The full issue is devoted to a description of the very first annual training seminar in 1977.

BIBLIOGRAPHY

Ardis, Susan B. *An Introduction to U.S. Patent Searching: The Process* (Englewood, Colorado: Libraries Unlimited, 1991).

Brown, Eulalie W. "Patent Basics: History, Background, and Searching Fundamentals," *Government Information Quarterly* 3 (4): 381-405 (1986).

Carpenter, Brian. "The U.S. Patent and Trademark Office Fellowship: A Note," *Journal of Government Information* 24 (2): 119-126 (1997).

Harwell, K.R. "Legal Issues Relating to Patent Searching in Publicly Accessible Libraries," *Journal of Government Information* 25 (1): 31-46 (1998).

Harwell, K.R. "Patent Searching: Core Collection and Suggestions for Service," *Reference Services Review* 21 (3): 49-60 (1993).

Harwell, K.R. "Report on Patent Depository Library Conference," *DttP (Documents to the People)* 19: 185-188 (1991).

Harwell, K.R. "Report on Patent Depository Library Conference," *DttP (Documents to the People)* 20: 176-180 (1992).

Thomas, Dena "Out of the Fire and Into the Frying Pan: Patent Reference Service in Non-Patent Depository Libraries," *The Reference Librarian* (32): 125-138 (1991). Also published in *Government Documents and Reference Services*, Robin Kinder, editor. (Binghamton, New York: Haworth Press, 1991).

Thomas, Dena. "Patent and Trademark Depository Library Conference XV," *Issues in Science and Technology Librarianship*, (2): unpaged–electronic journal (May 1992).

U.S. Patent and Trademark Office *Story of the U.S. Patent and Trademark Office* (Washington, DC: Government Printing Office, August 1988).

Wu, Connie and Calhoun, Ellen "Patents: A Valuable Resource in the Information Age," *Special Libraries* 83 (1): 16-24 (Winter 1992).

APPENDIX I. Current Map of PTDLs

PATENT AND TRADEMARK DEPOSITORY LIBRARIES

1. Akron, OH – Akron-Summit County Public Library
2. Albany, NY – New York State Library
3. Albuquerque, NM – Centennial Science and Engineering Library, University of New Mexico
4. Amherst, MA – Physical Sciences Library, University of Massachusetts
5. Anchorage, AK – Z.J. Loussac Public Library
6. Ann Arbor, MI – Engineering Library, University of Michigan
7. Atlanta, GA – Price Gilbert Memorial Library, Georgia Institute of Technology
8. Auburn University, AL – Ralph Brown Draughon Library
9. Austin, TX – McKinney Engineering Library, University of Texas at Austin
10. Baton Rouge, LA – Troy H. Middleton Library, Louisiana State University
11. Big Rapids, MI – Abigail S. Timme Library, Ferris State University
12. Birmingham, AL – Birmingham Public Library
13. Boston, MA – Boston Public Library
14. Buffalo, NY – Buffalo and Erie County Public Library
15. Burlington, VT – Bailey/Howe Library, University of Vermont
16. Butte, MT – Montana Tech Library of the University of Montana
17. Casper, WY – Natrona County Public Library
18. Chicago, IL – Chicago Public Library
19. Cincinnati, OH – The Public Library of Cincinnati and Hamilton County
20. Clemson, SC – R.M. Cooper Library, Clemson University
21. Cleveland, OH – Cleveland Public Library
22. College Park, MD – Engineering and Physical Sciences Library, University of Maryland
23. College Station, TX – Sterling C. Evans Library, Texas A&M University
24. Columbus, OH – Ohio State University Libraries
25. Concord, NH – New Hampshire State Library
26. Dallas, TX – Dallas Public Library
27. Denver, CO – Denver Public Library

28. Des Moines, IA – State Library of Iowa
29. Detroit, MI – Great Lakes Patent and Trademark Center, Detroit Public Library
30. Fort Lauderdale, FL – Broward County Main Library
31. Grand Forks, ND – Chester Fritz Library, University of North Dakota
32. Hartford CT – Hartford Public Library
33. Honolulu, HI – Hawaii State Public Library System
34. Houston, TX – The Fondren Library, Rice University
35. Indianapolis, IN – Indianapolis-Marion County Public Library
36. Jackson, MS – Mississippi Library Commission
37. Kansas City, MO – Linda Hall Library
38. Lincoln, NE – Engineering Library, University of Nebraska–Lincoln
39. Little Rock, AR – Arkansas State Library
40. Los Angeles, CA – Los Angeles Public Library
41. Louisville, KY – Louisville Free Public Library
42. Lubbock, TX – Texas Tech University Library
43. Madison, WI – Kurt F. Wendt Library, University of Wisconsin-Madison
44. Mayagüez, PR – General Library, University of Puerto Rico-Mayagüez
45. Memphis, TN – Memphis & Shelby County Public Library and Information Center
46. Miami, FL – Miami-Dade Public Library
47. Milwaukee, WI – Milwaukee Public Library
48. Minneapolis, MN – Minneapolis Public Library and Information Center
49. Morgantown, WV – Evansdale Library, West Virginia University
50. Moscow, ID – University of Idaho Library
51. Nashville, TN – Stevenson Science and Engineering Library, Vanderbilt University
52. New Haven, CT – New Haven Free Public Library
53. New York, NY – Science, Industry and Business Library, New York Public Library
54. Newark, DE – University of Delaware Library

55. Newark, NJ – Newark Public Library
56. Orono, ME – Raymond H. Fogler Library, University of Maine
57. Orlando, FL – University of Central Florida Library
58. Philadelphia, PA – The Free Library of Philadelphia
59. Piscataway, NJ – Library of Science and Medicine, Rutgers University
60. Pittsburgh, PA – The Carnegie Library of Pittsburgh
61. Portland, OR – Paul L. Boley Law Library, Lewis & Clark College
62. Providence, RI – Providence Public Library
63. Raleigh, NC – D.H. Hill Library, North Carolina State University
64. Rapid City, SD – Devereaux Library, South Dakota School of Mines and Technology
65. Reno, NV – University of Nevada–Reno Library
66. Richmond, VA – Cabell Library, Virginia Commonwealth University
67. Sacramento, CA – California State Library
68. St. Louis, MO – St. Louis Public Library
69. Salt Lake City, UT – Marriott Library, University of Utah
70. San Diego, CA – San Diego Public Library
71. San Francisco, CA – San Francisco Public Library
72. Seattle, WA – Engineering Library, University of Washington
73. Springfield, IL – Illinois State Library
74. Stillwater, OK – Center for International Trade Development, Oklahoma State University
75. Stony Brook, NY – Engineering Library, SUNY at Stony Brook
76. Sunnyvale, CA – Sunnyvale Center for Innovation, Invention and Ideas
77. Tampa, FL – University of South Florida Library
78. Tempe, AZ – Daniel E. Noble Science and Engineering Library, Arizona State University
79. Toledo, OH – Toledo/Lucas County Public Library
80. University Park, PA – Pattee Library, Pennsylvania State University
81. Washington, DC – Founders Library, Howard University
82. West Lafayette, IN – Siegesmund Engineering Library, Purdue University
83. Wichita, KS – Ablah Library, Wichita State University

☐ City or City/County Public Library
◯ College or University Library
◯ State Library
◯ Special Library

PTDLP

UNITED STATES DEPARTMENT OF COMMERCE
PATENT AND TRADEMARK OFFICE
PATENT AND TRADEMARK DEPOSITORY LIBRARY PROGRAM

June 1996

The Patent and Trademark Depository Library Program consists of 83 Patent and Trademark Depository Libraries (PTDLs) in the 50 states, the District of Columbia, and Puerto Rico. Call ahead of your visit for hours of operation, services, and fees.

Alabama	*	Auburn University: Ralph Brown Draughton Library	334-844-1747
		Birmingham Public Library	205-226-3620
Alaska		Anchorage: Z.J. Loussac Public Library, Anchorage Municipal Libraries	907-562-7323
Arizona	*	Tempe: Noble Science and Engineering Library, Arizona State University	602-965-7010
Arkansas	*	Little Rock: Arkansas State Library	501-682-2053
California	*	Los Angeles Public Library	213-228-7220
		Sacramento: California State Library	916-654-0069
		San Diego Public Library	619-236-5813
	*	San Francisco Public Library	415-557-4500
	**	Sunnyvale Center for Innovation, Invention & Ideas	408-730-7290
Colorado		Denver Public Library	303-640-6220
Connecticut		Hartford Public Library	860-543-8628
		New Haven Free Public Library	203-946-8130
Delaware		Newark: University of Delaware Library	302-831-2965
District of Columbia		Washington: Founders Library, Howard University	202-806-7252
Florida	*	Fort Lauderdale: Broward County Main Library	954-357-7444
	*	Miami-Dade Public Library	305-375-2665
		Orlando: University of Central Florida Libraries	407-823-2562
		Tampa Campus Library, University of South Florida	813-974-2726
Georgia		Atlanta: Library & Information Center, Georgia Institute of Technology	404-894-4508
Hawaii	*	Honolulu: Hawaii State Library	808-586-3477
Idaho		Moscow: University of Idaho Library	208-885-6235
Illlinois		Chicago Public Library	312-747-4450
		Springfield: Illinois State Library	217-782-5659
Indiana		Indianapolis-Marion County Public Library	317-269-1741
		West Lafayette: Siegesmund Engineering Library, Purdue University	765-494-2872
Iowa		Des Moines: State Library of Iowa	515-281-4118
Kansas	*	Wichita: Ablah Library Wichita State University	316-978-3155
Kentucky	*	Louisville Free Public Library	502-574-1611
Louisiana		Baton Rouge: Troy H. Middleton Library, Louisiana State University	504-388-8875
Maine		Orono: Raymond H. Fogler Library, University of Maine	207-581-1678
Maryland		College Park: Engineering and Physical Sciences Library, University of MD	301-405-9157
Massachusetts		Amherst: Physical Sciences and Engineering Library, University of Massachusetts	413-545-1370
	*	Boston Public Library	617-536-5400 Ext. 265
Michigan		Ann Arbor: Media Union Library, The University of Michigan	313-647-5735
		Big Rapids: Abigail S. Timme Library, Ferris State University	616-592-3602
	**	Detroit: Great Lakes Patent and Trademark Center, Detroit Public Library	313-833-3379
Minnesota	*	Minneapolis Public Library & Information Center	612-630-6120
Mississippi		Jackson: Mississippi Library Commission	601-359-1036
Nevada		Reno: University Library, University of Nevada-Reno	702-784-6500 Ext. 257
New Hampshire		Concord: New Hampshire State Library	603-271-2239
New Jersey		Newark Public Library of	973-733-7779
		Piscataway: Library of Science and Medicine, Rutgers University	732-445-2895
New Mexico		Albuquerque: Centennial Science and Engineering Library, The University of New Mexico	505-277-4412
New York		Albany: New York State Library	518-474-5355
	*	Buffalo and Erie County Public Library	716-858-7101
		New York: Science, Industry and Business Library, New York Public Library	212-592-7000
		Stony Brook: Engineering Library State University of New York	516-632-7148
North Carolina	*	Raleigh: D.H. Hill Library, North Carolina State University	919-515-2935
North Dakota		Grand Forks: Chester Fritz Library, University of North Dakota	701-777-4888
Ohio		Akron-Summit County Public Library	330-643-9075
		Cincinatti: The Public Library of Cincinnati and Hamilton County	513-369-6971
	*	Cleveland Public Library	216-623-2870
		Columbus: Ohio State University Libraries	614-292-6175
	*	Toledo/Lucas County Public Library	419-259-5212
Oklahoma	*	Stillwater: Oklahoma State University	405-744-7086
Oregon		Portland: Lewis & Clark College	503-768-6786
Pennsylvania	*	Philadelphia: The Free Library of	215-686-5331
		Pittsburgh: The Carnegie Library of	412-622-3138
		University Park: Pattee Library, Pennsylvania State University	814-865-4861
Puerto Rico		Mayagüez: General Library, University of Puerto Rico	787-832-4040 Ext. 3459
Rhode Island		Providence Public Library	401-455-8027
South Carolina		Clemson: R.M. Cooper Library, Clemson University	864-656-3024
South Dakota		Rapid City: Devereaux Library, South Dakota School of Mines and Technology	605-394-1275
Tennessee		Memphis & Shelby County Public Library & Information Center	901-725-8877
		Nashville: Stevenson Science and Engineering Library, Vanderbilt University	615-322-2717
Texas		Austin: McKinney Engineering Library, The University of Texas at Austin	512-495-4500
	*	College Station: Sterling C. Evans Library, Texas A&M University	409-845-3826
	*	Dallas Public Library	214-670-1468
	**	Houston: The Fondren Library, Rice University	713-527-8101 Ext. 2587
		Lubbock: Texas Tech University Library	806-742-2282
Utah	*	Salt Lake City: Marriott Library, University of Utah	801-581-8394
Vermont		Burlington: Bailey/Howe Library, University of Vermont	802-656-2542
Virginia	*	Richmond: James Branch Cabell Library, VA Commonwealth University	804-828-1104

APPENDIX I (continued)

Missouri	*	Kansas City: Linda Hall Library	816-363-4600	Washington	*	Seattle: Engineering Library, 206-543-0740
	*	St. Louis Public Library	314-241-2288			University of Washington
			Ext. 390	West Virginia	*	Morgantown: Evansdale Library, 304-293-2510
Montana		Butte: Montana Tech of the	406-496-4281			West Virginia University Ext. 5113
		University of Montana Library		Wisconsin		Madison: Kurt F. Wendt Library, 608-262-6845
Nebraska	*	Lincoln: Engineering Library,	402-472-3411			University of Wisconsin-Madison
		University of Nebraska-Lincoln				Milwaukee Public Library 414-286-3051
				Wyoming		Casper: Natrona County Public
						Library 307-237-4935

* Denotes APS-Text Access   ** Denotes Partnership PTDL

PTDL program information is also found on the Internet at **http://www.uspto.gov**

APPENDIX II
PTDL Fellowship Librarians
1983-1998

1st Fellowship
James A. Arshem
Denver Public Library
August 1, 1983-July 31, 1985

2nd Fellowship
Bruce B. Cox
Linda Hall Library
Kansas City, MO
October 1,1986-October 31,1987

3rd Fellowship
Linda J. Terhune
St. Louis Public Library
October 19,1987-October 18,1988

4th Fellowship
Jeanne L. Oliver
Illinois State Library, Springfield
October 17,1988-June 17,1990

5th Fellowship
Jean M. Porter
D.H. Hill Library
North Carolina State University, Raleigh
October 1,1989-December 31,1990

6th Fellowship
Chris E. Marhenke
Broward County Main Library
Ft. Lauderdale, FL
February 4,1991-August 1,1992

7th Fellowship
M. Neil Massong
Detroit Public Library
April 1,1991-April 1,1993

8th Fellowship
Brian B. Carpenter
Sterling C. Evans Library
Texas A & M University
September 1,1992-September 1, 1994

9th Fellowship
Marie Moisdon
Broward County Main Library
Ft. Lauderdale, FL
July 6,1993-July 6,1994

10th Fellowship
Erich J. Mayer
Buffalo and Erie County Public Library
August 29,1994-August 29,1995

11th Fellowship
Donna J. Cooper
Los Angeles Public Library
September 27,1994-September 27,1995

12th Fellowship
Carol A. Giles
St. Louis Public Library
February 19,1996-May 23,1997

13th Fellowship
David L. Morrison
Marriott Library
University of Utah, Salt Lake City
October 28,1996-October 28,1997

14th Fellowship
Michael J. White
Raymond H. Fogler Library
University of Maine, Orono
June 30,1997-June 29,1998

15th Fellowship
Charlotte Erdmann
Siegesmund Engineering Library
Purdue University
West Lafayette, IN
July 1, 1998-

16th Fellowship
Thomas A. Turner
Daniel E. Noble Science and Engineering
Library
Arizona State University, Tempe
November 9,1998 -

Training, a Library Imperative

Glen E. Holt

SUMMARY. To build a bright future for our libraries, we have to get training right. Modern, high-tech, customer-service driven libraries must train and train and train. Training, like so many other management tools, has become a library spending imperative. It is one of the library director's sharpest tools for directing shifts in institutional culture and speeding changes in work and customer service. Training is paramount because only a few persons among the hundreds employed are fully prepared to work for us when they are first hired. *[Article copies available for a fee from The Haworth Document Delivery Service: 1-800-342-9678. E-mail address: getinfo@haworthpressinc.com <Website: http://www.haworthpressinc.com>]*

KEYWORDS. Staff training, training of employees, library skills, evaluation

THE TRAINING IMPERATIVE

I just finished a fifteen-month consulting stint with a large urban library system. The observations I share in the next few paragraphs are included in my final report and oral reports delivered to a library board, local legislators and in public meetings. What I say here, therefore, is public information.

This system is stuck in an idiosyncratic "books and buildings" syndrome that is out of touch with what area citizens want–as deter-

---

Glen E. Holt is Executive Director, St. Louis Public Library.

[Haworth co-indexing entry note]: "Training, a Library Imperative." Holt, Glen E. Co-published simultaneously in *Journal of Library Administration* (The Haworth Information Press, an imprint of The Haworth Press, Inc.) Vol. 29, No. 1, 1999, pp. 79-93; and: *Library Training for Staff and Customers* (ed: Sara Ramser Beck) The Haworth Information Press, an imprint of The Haworth Press, Inc., 2000, pp. 79-93. Single or multiple copies of this article are available for a fee from The Haworth Document Delivery Service [1-800-342-9678, 9:00 a.m. - 5:00 p.m. (EST). E-mail address: getinfo@haworthpressinc.com].

mined by numerous community meetings, multiple focus groups and a statistically reliable telephone survey. Problems are seething. Staff morale is low. Major technology investment is behind the curve. Every staff member is rightfully worried about the system's future. Organizational communication up, down and sideways is weak throughout the system. Change resisters dominate many work units.

As one important change, I recommended that this library vastly increase training. Training, after all, is the principal tool for changing institutional culture. Training prepares staff for change. Training helps workers and work units learn new ways of doing their work. Training sets the tone of customer service. How can any modern library not make training a budget priority?

A few weeks after completing the library's new strategic plan, I asked the organization's chief financial officer how much training money was in the FY1999 budget. "Less than $10,000," he said. "There's just too much else to do."

There's a street term for such management behavior: Urban youth say, "He dissed me!" The "dis" is for "disrespected." A library system that makes training a low priority disrespects the staff who work there. Staff have a right to expect regular and substantial training so they can do their jobs better. Ignoring training sends a clear message: The staff isn't worth it! No training or token training is "dissing" the staff.

To build a bright future for our libraries, we have to get training right. Modern, high-tech, customer-service-driven libraries must train and train and train. Library managers who cannot find generous budget support for training are still living in the old-fashioned world where library schools taught "library writing," where well-educated, cheap-waged "nice girls" worked until they got married and where the Internet, mega-bookstores, Amazon.com and expectations of high customer service did not exist as strategic realities.

Training, like so many other management tools, has become a library spending imperative. It is one of the library director's sharpest tools for directing shifts in institutional culture and speeding changes in work and customer service.

TRAINING FOR THE JOB

It is almost impossible to attend a library function in the United States without some director trotting out the old cliche about having "the best staff." In this happy-talk litany, staff are portrayed as exemplars of miracle skills and fabulous motivation, "self-sacrificing professionals" who are aided by eager minions who smilingly "pitch in to get the job done."

Within these enthusiastic criteria, my staff IS NOT a "great staff."

My staff IS a "high-performance staff," and I have some statistics to back up that claim. The St. Louis Public Library (SLPL) staff is one that returns to its users $4 in direct benefits for every $1 in public tax support.[1] Users who estimate these benefits say that their contacts with staff make up a big percentage–more than 40 percent–of the value they get from using the library. Another indicator of high performance is seen in changing output measures. As all of SLPL's measures have doubled or tripled through the last decade, staff numbers have increased only 30 percent. SLPL has many "good jobs." There are not many of them where the staff member does not leave at the end of the day realizing that she/he works for a living.

Our high performance staff is no accident.

It comes, first, from a solid recruitment program that stresses diversity and a work organization that generally provides a good deal of latitude for initiative and self-actualization within a framework of meeting institutional goals that carry out the library's mission.

Second, this high performance staff also works in a "pure merit" salary system that can reward outstanding job performance with higher salaries. That system, developed over many years, is coupled with an on-going effort to remove the unmotivated and low performers from the employment setting.

And, third, this high-performance staff is dependent on training.

That training is paramount because only a few among the hundreds we employ are prepared to work for us when they walk in the door. That is true through the ranks. New recruits are mostly nice human beings who have had an enormous variety of life experiences and who are moving at various speeds along many different personal "roads to somewhere." Their prior training reflects all the weaknesses and strengths of public and private K-12 education, myriad collegiate experiences and the vagaries of MLIS professional instruction.

Four out of ten shelving applicants fail our alphabetical/decimal test that marks minimal qualification for hiring. With 35 percent of our city's adults without functional workplace literacy, we must check on reading ability even in housekeeping jobs to make sure candidates can read cleaning-product labels.

In more than a decade we never have hired a maintenance person who was ready to handle the diverse and specialized requirements of our 17 buildings and our fleet of vans and trucks. And, no matter how good the qualifications of those we hire as clerks and paraprofessionals, they must be prepared to perform our work tasks the way we want them done.

Professional librarians present more complex training problems. Few new MLS degree holders are ready for our workplace. One newly minted cataloguer whom we hired half a decade ago represented the worst of the lot. Arriving for the first day's work, the new hire's supervisor seated the person at a desk filled with stacks of procedural manuals and stated that mastering these was the start of handling the regular workload. At noon, the neophyte came to the supervisor and said, "I quit! I just got my degree. I don't need to know all of this stuff."

The best of the newly-minted library professionals, even those with prior work experience and a degree in a subject area, often are weak in handling difficult customer-service problems, on-line searching, staff supervision, coaching and/or disciplining employees, intra-organizational communication, budgeting and financial management. Moreover, many find the collegial give and take of purposeful work hard to handle. As one of our youth services professionals says, "Many arrive not knowing how to play nicely with the other children."

Even more training is needed in high-level management. Along with the items on the list in the prior paragraph, system and unit administrators have to recognize the difference between authority and the span of control on the one hand and organizational power and influence on the other. Moreover, at the top of the organization, administrators have to manage "the clash of cultures" between professional librarians on one side and professionals in community relations, electronic communications, computers, facilities, finance, fund raising, human resources, marketing and security on the other.[2] At the top of any organization, substantial training is necessary to avoid both the "Peter Principle" and "burn out."

Library staff require a variety of formal and informal training, beginning with orientation to the organizational culture, continuing with specialty training for success in highly differentiated work tasks, communicating within and across units to help the whole organization carry out its mission, and, hardly least in importance, keeping up with change. An example of the latter: Most librarians are trained to do in-person reference interviews, but the reference business will become increasingly virtual. Another: Most librarians are trained to handle "library orientation" for their users, but the "library training" that users most want today is how to use computers. The demand for this public training ranges from what we have come to call "Mousing 101" to very specialized database searching well beyond the expertise of most librarians, especially those educated before the age of networked computing.

Training is an imperative–to make staff successful and to make our libraries successful in carrying out their missions.

WHERE TO START

The place to begin improving a training program is to find out what needs to be done, then deciding what needs to be done first. Simple informal surveys of staff, whether written on forms, answers to e-mail questions or discussions around a table, can bring training needs into the open.

SLPL's most recent training agenda developed out of a mid-1990s administration decision to see if all staff would buy into the development of an institutional values statement. Facilitated by outside experts in group process, the development of the institutional values statement turned into a rich learning experience–and a revealing one about how much all staff wanted more training in order to do their jobs better. At the conclusion of the values exercise, the facilitators presented to administration a long list of training needs that staff had articulated during their participation in the activity. These recommendations became the basis for the next round of SLPL training put in place over several years.

INSTITUTIONAL TRAINING GOALS

I have derived the following set of SLPL training goals from the SLPL Mission Statement, the institutional values statement and the training courses offered through the past two years. If I repeated this exercise in two or five years, I know that I would write it differently because the institution would require a different training emphasis. These are the current institutional training goals. Training should help staff:

1. Do their individual jobs better.
2. Create/maintain a positive work environment in all units.
3. Create/maintain a welcoming environment for the public.
4. Work effectively together, within own unit and with other unit teams.
5. Recognize that we learn from each other.
6. Recognize that cooperation works better than competition within the organization.
7. Treat other staff with the courtesy expected from them.
8. Build individual job skills no matter where located in the organization.
9. Embrace change as a positive.
10. Demonstrate continuing willingness to improve personal performance.

SLPL-U

When SLPL's Central Library opened in 1912, one whole wing of one floor was designated as "Training Rooms." The old curriculum centered on book mending, binding, cataloging, catalog card copying, materials ordering, check-out procedures, and shelving, to name only course entries that appeared the most frequently. As library schools proliferated and as SLPL went through two different financial downturns, this training grew less extensive. Finally the old training rooms were given over to collections holdings and public service.

Through the last twelve years, I have increased staff training often. Training now is so pervasive within the organization that I have started talking about it as "SLPL-U." The curriculum of SLPL-U and most other large urban libraries is too extensive to replicate here. As work changes, the training emphases shift. Here are the principal categories of training with some illustrations.

1. Computer-based work, including word processing/spread-sheets/ Windows, Internet and database searching and DRA functions

and procedures. Special training given to staff, youth and public use policies for the Internet.
2. Communication and team building, including oral and written communication, conflict resolution and media-interview techniques.
3. Public services, including those delivered over the phone and electronically. Training courses include the Phone Doctor, handling mentally disturbed persons and other problem patrons.
4. Library skills. Old stand-bys include reference, reader's advisory and working flexibly within library-use policies. Subject area training and unit orientation help staff to handle reference and make successful referrals.
5. Safety, including driving, workplace environment, staff health (staff sick at work, AIDS in the workplace) and disaster management.
6. Security training, including personal safety, use of security staff, and how to handle and report security incidents.
7. Effective use of staff resources, including team reference, cross-training, best referrals, and use of new worker categories like homework helpers and technology assistants. Working with volunteers also has become important training in many work units.
8. Management training, including priority setting, use of authority, team building, making out purchase orders, and handling annual appraisals. Upper level managers have had media training as well.
9. Training the public in library use, especially how to use computers, the Internet and electronic databases. Many other course listings could be included. The training program is extensive, and it is ongoing.

WHO SHOULD MANAGE TRAINING

In American corporations, most training is organized by human resources (HR) professionals. That is not necessarily true in libraries. At an Urban Libraries Council seminar on staff training a few years ago, the sixty institutions at the conference mostly centered their training in HR, but these offices were as frequently headed by librarians as by HR specialists.

By intent SLPL training management is dispersed through the organization. Since SLPL is so deeply involved with computers and networks, until recently, the designated head of SLPL training was the library's Webmaster. Because we needed greater institutional technology leadership from the Webmaster, a few weeks ago, the head of branch services, who had been deeply involved in training, moved from her old slot to become manager of training. The head of HR, who also manages security and housekeeping, handles all initial library orientation and watches over support-service training and the general staff training associated with the areas he supervises.

The head of customer services conducts ongoing training for shelvers, circulation clerks and all public service staff and most librarians on library policies and procedures. The head of Central manages the training and cross-training of reference and subject specialists. All unit heads train and/or organize training for the specialties of their units.

INFORMAL TRAINING

In addition, there is informal training. A recent study by the Center for Workforce Development of Newton, Massachusetts, reinforces good library work practices. The study brought teams of psychologists to seven manufacturing corporations to survey and dissect company cultures.

Researchers found that during a typical workweek, more than seventy percent of work site training took place informally, with employees sharing information with one another. "Fifty-five percent of the respondents said they asked co-workers, not supervisors, for advice," the study noted. Overall, informal training was found to be continuous, if often unrecognized; instead of being a drain on productivity, so-called idle chatter was actually good for business."

The study noted, however, that the value of "informal training" is enhanced by formal staff training. More high quality information about institutional procedures and training in how to communicate within the organizational culture adds value, because employees need "more information and more open communication to do their jobs better."[3] I recognize this strong relationship between formal and informal learning as a critical component in the SLPL training program.

TRAINING THE TRAINERS

Several years ago, we brought together two dozen unit heads to train them as trainers. The instructors for these sessions were experts in group facilitation and adult education. These professionals helped our librarian-trainers recognize that good training should not consist of replicating bad college lectures. The trainers pointed out the importance of hands-on learning, of having learners actively involved in training exercises and the significance of varying learning activities within the same session. In short, the outside trainers helped staff trainers recognize that effective training for working adults, no matter what their educational levels, has to be active in nature and focused on helping workers make immediate improvements in their work. This adult education emphasis remains a feature of SLPL formal training.

THE COSTS OF TRAINING

Obviously, a substantial training program costs something. But how much should a library spend for training? How much is enough?[4]

A recent survey in the printing industry, which, like libraries, constitutes a knowledge business, reported that about fifty percent of all printing companies spent $250 or less annually to train each employee; thirty-one percent of the companies spent $251 to $750 annually; and eighteen percent spent over $1,000. In the same survey, fifty-five percent provided all training on company time, while forty-three percent trained on a combination of paid and unpaid time.[5]

A more recent survey of American companies with fifty or more employees provides another cost benchmark for training expenses. An American Society for Training and Development survey showed that all such companies spend $58 billion annually on formal training. That amounts to about $500 for each employee annually, with sixty-seven percent going for salaries of in-house trainers or fees of outside professionals.[6]

One important part of determining costs is deciding what to include in the calculation. Andy Hubbard, a professional trainer in the banking industry, an information industry where employment and service models often resemble library organizations, writes: "[The] cost of training includes the purchase of research and development of training materials, instructor compensation, space allocation, capitalized equipment (PCs and audiovisual equipment), production of student materials, and other incidental materials."[7]

Hubbard says that two expenses ought to be excluded: "the cost of transportation to the class for remote participants, and the compensation of participants while they are in class." In the operating budgets of most libraries, this allocation would mean that transport to convention or conference locations would be excluded but the costs of seminar registration fees and materials would be included.

Using Hubbard's criteria, in FY1996, when I gathered my first full compilation of SLPL training costs, we were spending close to $150,000 for training. That amounted to about 2 percent of the institution's total salary line. In FY1999, the total training figure moved well over $300,000, or something more than 4 percent of all SLPL salaries. In the same three-year period, the cost to train all full-time (and full-time equivalent) employees on average has risen from about $585 each to over $1,100 each.

I have checked out the 4 percent-to-5 percent of salary-line figure with several directors of other large urban libraries. A number of such institutions, especially if they are in a period of technological transformation, are expending similar percentages of their budgets on training.

TRAINING COSTS FORM AN INVERTED PYRAMID

This average cost conceals an inverted pyramid of training expense.

Everyone in the organization needs training. To avoid customer-service problems and even lawsuits, housekeeping staff need special training in manipulating chemicals, using equipment and learning how to lift. Receiving and delivery require training in routing routines, loading and lifting, along with special safe-driving instruction. To save money, maintenance people need certification in specialties like HVAC and preventative maintenance routines. The latter usually is computer-based. Clerks and paraprofessionals throughout the system need training in special routines and customer service, including dealing with inappropriate behavior and angry patrons. The list goes on and on. No one in the SLPL system, including the executive director, escapes training for very long. Throughout the organization, training is the tool to build teams, develop better staff morale and help individuals and groups work more efficiently and effectively.

TRAINING OF UPPER-LEVEL MANAGERS

No group requires more constant and specialized training than those at the top of the organization–starting with directors and including all top-level managers. I have put my management team and myself in classes with any number of team-building trainers, financial management trainers, space planning and building design management trainers, technology management trainers and electronic-communication trainers–and those categories don't begin to cover all of the training that we have experienced singly and together. Obviously, such training is not cheap, but if the management team doesn't perform well, the rest of the library is likely to be a mess. So the cost is justified.

TRAINING FOR LIBRARY PROFESSIONALS

After upper-level management, the next-highest cost on a per-person basis is that for training professional librarians. Some of this training is to do old things in new ways. Some of it is so that librarians can do new things the best way.

Reference training is the place to begin. Training always improves mediocre reference performance. And without training, reference performance is often mediocre. One detailed four-year reference training experience raised observed reference accuracy from 42.5 percent accurate to 97.5 percent accurate.[8] That change is one worth emulating.

Training in reader's advisory is next. Reader's advisory in most libraries reminds me of faculty behavior in large academic departments in American universities: In those departments, each professor often is the master of such specialized knowledge that communication among the individuals except at the most basic methodological level is difficult at best. Mary K. Chelton in a recent article shows how much has to be done to improve reader's advisory service.[9]

The individualistic reader's advisory nexus can be changed. Technological tools like OCLC's Fiction Project and CARL's NoveList are helping to bring discussions of reader's advisory center-stage in public library training agendas. SLPL is working to help solve this training problem. Library staff from St. Louis is partnered with Duncan Smith, who created NoveList, to develop standard protocols that can be used in reader's advisory training. Another benefit of this partnership is the development of library practices by which staff develop "reader communities" around heavily read popular books.

TECHNOLOGY TRAINING

Over the past decade, many SLPL librarians have had to learn basic keyboarding, word processing, spread sheets, search procedures for two different automated catalogs, Internet searching and online searching of single and multiple databases. In the process, they have had to master the functional quirks of the architecture and operating systems of the 286, 386, and 486, along with Pentium I and Pentium II. In the meantime, they have worked in a world that has gone from entirely book-oriented reference work to database-focused reference with paper supplements when current information is either unavailable or not needed.

RESISTANCE TO TRAINING
AND THE CHANGE IT SYMBOLIZES

Do all staff want this training? Not all, by any means. Some library staff–including high-level managers–resist training just as they resist change generally. Like almost all training groups, librarians in training break down into "eager adopters, prove-its and resisters." That makes them typical rather than exceptions.

"The majority of people have low tolerance for *any* change," says Paul Kazmierski, an industrial psychologist and professor at Rochester Institute of Technology in Rochester, New York. "If employees don't understand the reason for change and they aren't involved in planning for it, they're going to resist it."[10]

A special librarian who heads an information-resource center for a Canadian KPMG financial advising and consulting firm with international clients wrote of her electronic training experiences this way.[11]

> Information professionals may encounter obstacles to their undertaking training responsibilities. One roadblock encountered is the belief that information professionals should not be Internet trainers. . . .
>
> Time can be another obstacle. . . . One hundred and fifty (or more) hours preparation per one hour of instruction is not unusual.
>
> Ignorance can also have an impact. Many Internet users doubt they need additional training. It's up to you to show them what they're missing. . . .

Participants will be overloaded and will remember only a small amount of the information you've shown them. . . .

Don't be upset if you don't get it right the first time. . . . Successful training programs are 50 percent material and 50 percent presenter.

The time and materials investment involved in producing Internet training programs can put a strain on the library resources, but ignoring the opportunities and falling behind also has a price tag. When all is said and done, you want participants to go away with knowledge and skills that will make them better able to function when you're not there.

This last point is especially important. The ultimate purpose of training is staff empowerment–giving them the tools to do their job better. Not to train is to disrespect staff.

EVALUATION OF TRAINING OUTCOMES

The outcomes of training need to be evaluated. This evaluation can take many forms.

One is testing. As SLPL adopts a new automation system after more than a decade operating the old one, we are testing staff on their readiness to perform system functions. I decided we needed to test staff on functional capability because during our first automation migration I saw how dependent some staff were on other staff to get them through even the most basic automated computer routines. This "training lag" in come cases lasted for weeks. Through the past decade, our users have come to expect greater technological proficiency from staff. Simple testing is a way to make sure that staff can meet those high customer expectations.

Outside evaluators also have a place in evaluating training. Dr. Leslie Edmonds Holt, Director of Youth Services and Family Literacy at SLPL, is using outside evaluators to measure the effectiveness of the child reading-readiness instruction training her staff is giving to other library staff, the staff of daycare centers and parents. This research and its evaluation is being funded by a Department of Education grant.[12] The project's evaluation component was a very important reason for the grant.

Not long ago librarian Carrie Russell reported a successful "performance measurement" evaluation of team training at the University of

Arizona Library in Tucson. As Russell wrote, this evaluation method was right for what was being taught. "A team-based environment needs an evaluation system that honors, evaluates and rewards team performance," she concluded. This mechanism had an additional function: to serve as a feedback mechanism so that the team could adapt on an ongoing basis to continuous change.[13]

THE BENEFITS OF TRAINING EXPENDITURE

For the past three years SLPL has been engaged in a formal cost-benefit analysis to estimate the benefits its users get from public tax investment in library services.[14] That study, as reported in a recent *Library Journal* article, showed that SLPL users derived a greater share of benefits from their interaction with well-trained staff than from any other materials and service category.[15] In September 1998, the Institute for Museum and Library Services made a substantial grant to SLPL to develop its cost-benefit analysis methodology into one that can be used by other large urban libraries.[16] Checking the user benefits derived from customer interaction with well-trained staff will be one important feature of the study.

The policy implication of the staff-benefits section of the SLPL cost-benefit analysis (CBA) study is that no library can sustain its reputation as a customer-oriented information-and-knowledge institution without a major investment in staff training. Such training needs to be formal as well as informal, and effective effort needs to be made to measure the fact that staff training has had the desired impact. I believe the national CBA study will confirm this finding for other urban public libraries.

This brief discussion of CBA brings this paper back to its beginning: A solid staff-training program is an operational imperative for an effective bottom line in the 21st-century library.

NOTES

1. Glen E. Holt, Donald Elliott and Amonia Moore. Placing a value on public library services. A St. Louis case study. *Public Libraries*, forthcoming; Glen E. Holt and Donald Elliott, Proving your library's worth: A test case. *Library Journal*, 123: 18 (November 1, 1998), pp. 42-44.

2. Joseph A. Raelin, *The clash of cultures: Managers and professionals*. Boston: Harvard Business School Press, 1986. Raelin focuses on the clash between managers and technologists, but his discussion is highly relevant to the problems of operating a large urban library.

3. Forget the formal training, *Library Administrator's Digest*, 33: 7 (September 1998), p. 49. This article highlights a much longer article in the *New York Times*, May 10, 1998.

4. This section is based on Glen E. Holt, Staff training: How much is enough. *The Bottom Line*, 9:1(1996), pp. 43-44.

5. Holt, pp. 43-44.

6. Forget the formal training, p. 49.

7. Holt, pp. 43-44.

8. Lillie Seward Dyson. Improving reference services: A Maryland training program brings positive results. (September/October 1992), pp. 284-289.

9. Mary K. Chelton, What we know and don't know about reading, readers, and readers advisory services. *Public Libraries*, 38:1 (January-February, 1999), pp. 42-47.

10. Shari Caudron. The human side of a technology launch. *Training and Development* (February 1997), pp. 21-24.

11. Hope A. Bell. The librarian as trainer: Internet training–Lessons learned. *Information Outlook,* (April 1998), pp. 17-20.

12. St. Louis Public Library. Project REAL: Developing a family literacy service-St. Louis Public Library. US Department of Education, Office of Research and Improvement, Library Research and Demonstration Program, Grant Application.

13. Carrie Russell. Using performance measurement to evaluate teams and organizational effectiveness. *Library Administration & Management*, 12:3 (Summer 1998), pp. 159-165.

14. Holt, Elliott & Moore, forthcoming.

15. Holt & Elliott, pp. 42-44.

16. St. Louis Public Library, Library cost benefit analysis. Washington: Institute for Museum and Library Services, 1998 IMLS National Leadership Grant Application.

Index

**FACULTY: THIS SPECIAL ISSUE IS AVAILABLE
FOR ADOPTION IN A FULLY INDEXED
SEPARATELY BOUND TEXTBOOK EDITION!**

*An excellent resource that will help your students
learn to educate staff and customers in the use
of new library technology!*

NEW!

LIBRARY TRAINING
FOR STAFF AND CUSTOMERS

Edited by
Sara Ramser Beck, MLS, MBA
Manager, Business, Science, and Technology
Department, St. Louis Public Library,
St. Louis, Missouri

This comprehensive textbook is designed
to assist future library professionals
who will be involved in presenting
or planning training for library staff
members and customers. It explores
ideas for effective general reference
training, training on automated systems,
training in specialized subjects such as
African-American history and biography,
and training for areas such as patents
and trademarks, and business subjects.
**Library Training for Staff and
Customers** answers numerous training
questions and is an excellent guide for
planning staff development.

Contents
* More Than Meets the Eye: Management
  Support for Reference Service and
  Training

* Technology Training at the St. Louis
  Public Library

* Training Staff for Business Reference

* A Model Workshop to Increase Knowledge
  of African-American Reference Sources for
  Public Services Library Staff

* Fully Disclosed Yet Merely Descriptive:
  intricacies of Training the Patient and
  Trademark Information Professional

* Training, A Library Imperative

* Reference Notes Included

* Index

(A monograph published simultaneously as the
Journal of Library Administration,
Vol. 29, No. 1.)
$39.95 hard. ISBN: 0-7890-0965-X.
(Outside US/Canada/Mexico: $48.00)
$24.95 soft. ISBN: 0-7890-0983-8.
(Outside US/Canada/Mexico: $30.00)
2000. Available now. 108 pp. with Index.

The Haworth Information Press
An imprint of The Haworth Press, Inc.
10 Alice Street
Binghamton, New York 13904-1580 USA

FTO/00